THE SPIRITUAL ART
OF DIALOGUE

THE SPIRITUAL ART OF DIALOGUE

Mastering Communication for
Personal Growth, Relationships,
and the Workplace

ROBERT APATOW, Ph.D.

Inner Traditions
Rochester, Vermont

Inner Traditions International
One Park Street
Rochester, Vermont 05767
www.gotoit.com

Library of Congress Cataloging-in-Publication Data
Apatow, Robert, 1966–
The spiritual art of dialogue : mastering communication for personal
growth, relationships, and the workplace / Robert Apatow.
p.   cm.
Includes bibliographical references and index.
ISBN 0-89281-674-0 (hardcover : alk. paper)
1. Dialogue analysis.   I. Title.
P95.455.A68 1998   98-9213
302.2'24—dc21   CIP

Printed and bound in the United States

10   9   8   7   6   5   4   3   2   1

Text design and layout by Virginia L. Scott
This book was typeset in Minion with Wade Sans Light as the display typeface

Distributed to the book trade in Canada by Publishers Group West (PGW),
Toronto
Distributed to the book trade in the United Kingdom by Deep Books, London
Distributed to the book trade in Australia by Gemcraft Books, Burwood
Distributed to the book trade in New Zealand by Tandem Press, Auckland
Distributed to the book trade in South Africa by Alternative Books, Ferndale

And if the questioner were one of the wise logic choppers who argue only to win, I would say to him: "My position has been stated; if I do not reason correctly, it is your job to take hold of my statement and refute it." However, if such people should wish to enter into a dialogue with each other as friends, like you and I are now, it would be necessary for them to be somewhat more gentle and to answer each other in a manner more appropriate to the dialectic. And equally important, it is the more dialectical approach not only to answer the truth but also to answer by means of those things which the questioner would agree he does know. I will then also try to speak to you in this way. So reason with me.

Socrates
(from Plato's Meno)

CONTENTS

ACKNOWLEDGMENTS

This book emerges from my study of the dialogues of the Greek philosopher Plato. In this study I have especially benefited from my participation as a member of the Noetic Society, a nonprofit educational organization devoted to the study of Wisdom traditions. The Noetic Society is directed by my friend and teacher Dr. Pierre Grimes, who has revived the ancient Greek philosophy and is a true master of the art of dialogue. Pierre Grimes's life and work have been a model for both this book and my own philosophical growth. I would like to thank Dr. Grimes and Alan Hartley of *New Perspectives* magazine for allowing me to include a large part of Grimes's article "The Art of Delivering Oneself of False Beliefs." For those who are interested in learning more about Grimes's work, I highly recommend his books, which are cited in the bibliography, and encourage readers to visit his webpage located at philosophicalmidwifery.com.

I would like to thank all the people who provided comments and suggestions on earlier drafts of this book: Monique Apatow, Maury Apatow, Mark Bartholio, Kimberly Walsh, Joe Grimes, Yolanda McDonald, Samantha Shad, Molly Shad, Barry Goldberg, editor Jon Graham for his interest in this project, copy editor Marcia Merryman Means and editor Blake Maher for their very thoughtful suggestions, and the rest of the wonderful editorial staff at Inner Traditions. Finally, I owe a special thanks to my friend John Vivanco who first encouraged me to start this project.

PREFACE

What is this Book About?

Are there any established rules or accepted standards for the discussion of controversial questions and issues? Is there a better way to communicate with one another than the methods of arguing and debating that we are all familiar with and which usually get us nowhere? Is there a way for friends to explore interesting questions and issues without becoming angry with one another? A familiar adage warns us: "Two things friends ought never to discuss are politics and religion." The adage expresses the fear that if friends enter into such discussions, they may not long remain friends. Such a fear exists because we no longer possess the knowledge of how to confront our differences in discussion.

There does exist an approach to the exploration of ideas and issues, but it has been lost. This knowledge constitutes the art of dialogue that was central to the life and culture of the ancient Greeks. In the world of ancient Greece, friends did not avoid discussions of politics and religion, but instead sought them out as a most meaningful social activity. The Greeks were a philosophical culture that established principles for dialogue and cultivated it as an art. This book introduces this ancient approach to dialogue into our contemporary life and shows how to apply these principles in your everyday world. Dialogue offers us a remarkably powerful means toward personal growth. With the principles of dialogue you will be better prepared to deal with the challenges at your workplace and in your personal life. Dialogue is also an essential means through which to cultivate and enrich your relationships. This book also shows the way dialogue fits into the ancient Greek picture of the cosmos and explains how the wisdom of the ancients can help you better understand the drama of your own life.

INTRODUCTION

Dialogue literally means "through logos." In ancient Greek, *logos* means "word" but also "reason," because the realm of words is the abode of reasoning. Thus, for the Greeks, to have a dialogue is to share reasoning. When we enter into a dialogue and share reasoning, we relate through the world of ideas and have the opportunity to gain an understanding of one another. Although understanding is not a physical thing, it has a very real unifying power. with another. Therefore, dialogue offers an opportunity to unite with another, and the deeper the understanding, the greater the bond.

When we engage in dialogue, we enter into an intimate relationship with another human being. We express our lives in many different ways—in our appearance, our gestures, the way we walk, the choices we make, our decisions and actions—but the most direct and most revealing form of expression is through our words. When we communicate with another, we share our most private possession—our thoughts. Thoughts are the soul's speech with itself, and unlike everything else in the world (that is, things that are experienced through the five senses), our thoughts cannot be directly experienced by another—except through words.

When we express our thoughts to another in words, we express our minds and reveal who we truly are. From the start, then, dialogue poses a great challenge to us, for in dialogue we allow another to enter into this most solitary and private abode where our thoughts dwell. And when we open up in this way, we let ourselves be seen free of the cloak of any physical appearance; whatever appearance we may wear in life, the expression of our thoughts cuts right through it and reveals the truth about us. Understandably, this is a risky and fearful activity that demands great courage, but it is for these very reasons that dialogue is such a remarkably compelling activity. We all are drawn to such genuine intimate revelations. In such revelations there is a remarkable power and beauty that draws us—a power that manifests itself when someone is most sincere, genuine, and real. This is the power of Truth. Through dialogue we have a chance to see people as they truly are, and this is why dialogue presents the greatest means to personal and social growth.

In the ancient world, dialogue was pursued as an art. According to this classical vision, the nature of art is to seek the benefit of the subject of the particular art. Here the word *art* means a knowledge and power (not a creative talent, as in the contemporary use of the term). We continue to use this sense of art when we speak of things like the martial arts or the healing arts. The art of healing is a kind of knowledge that is possessed by a healer. The healer, or physician, aims to use this art to benefit her proper subject, one who is ill. Similarly, there is an art of the pilot. The pilot of a ship or an airplane uses his knowledge to convey passengers safely. The art or knowledge is never used to benefit the one who possesses the art, for he is not in need. For example, the healer does not seek her own benefit when functioning as a healer. She works to heal the patient. (However, the healer can heal herself and so play the role of healer and patient.) And so, according to the principles of an art, one who has the art can be compensated only for his time and not for his knowledge.

There exists an art of dialogue, and it was possessed by Socrates, the ancient Greek philosopher. This art has been revived by my teacher, the contemporary philosopher Pierre Grimes. The art of dialogue possesses a power to benefit individuals and looks toward its own ideal in its practice. Whereas the healer looks toward the ideal of health to benefit his patients, the master of dialogue looks toward the ideal of Truth, to help individuals distinguish truth from falsehood. This kind of dialogue was a spiritual practice of the ancient Greeks.

Dialogue possesses a remarkable power to effect personal and spiritual growth and can offer our world perhaps the greatest means for the healing and further evolution of society. The function of dialogue is to bring people together as friends in the shared exploration of the truth of an issue. Dialogue demands the most genuine sincerity and the greatest courage for people to face both the challenge of giving up what is false and of accepting what is true. It requires that people bring forth from themselves what is most reasonable and free of prejudice. And since it is a social activity, it demands that we express our deepest concern for one another and our respect for the principles of fairness that must govern personal relationships. Through dialogue we gain the opportunity to reason with another and to transcend the limitations of our personal beliefs and views. It exercises the highest part of our minds and awakens us to the potential of this distinctly human faculty of reason. In its highest form, dialogue challenges us to give up our prejudices and false beliefs and to allow the innate wisdom that all humans have the potential to share to come forth and express itself.

To master the art of dialogue is truly a lifetime study. Those who seek mastery of this art would be wise to take up the active study of the dialogues of Plato and his presentation of the greatest master of this art—Socrates. This book does not claim to lead people to this kind of mastery; instead, it presents an introduction to the fundamental principles of dialogue in such a way as to benefit people who in their everyday lives sincerely wish to improve their personal lives and help improve our world. At the same time, it will give the reader a rich introduction to a profound vision of the ancient Greek Wisdom tradition that is not only relevant but indeed essential for the future well-being of humankind.

The first chapter looks at the problem of communication in our society and introduces the simple rules that constitute the classical model of dialogue. The second chapter explores the ancient origins of this model and its relationship to Greek tragedy and philosophy and introduces the greatest master of dialogue—Socrates. Chapter three presents the structural elements of dialogue as a game, or form of play, that includes rules and players. The fourth chapter discusses the issue of truth. The goal of dialogue is to discover truth, but how can we answer skeptical challengers or the skeptical voices within ourselves? How can we respond to the objection that "it is all relative" and that there is no truth but only subjective opinions?

Chapter five takes up the personal element in dialogue, the inherent drama that accompanies dialogue, and the problem of roles, masks, and projections. It also begins the exploration of dialogue as a means to personal growth. The sixth chapter explores how one can engage in dialogue in the spirit of a Zen art, in which one aims to transcend the ego. The next chapter presents the dynamics of inner dialogue, that is, a dialogue with oneself, and also the principles for cultivating a dialogue with the source of intuition and wisdom within us. Chapter eight begins to reveal the ways in which we can apply the principles of dialogue to our love relationships and with our children. In the ninth chapter, we explore the application of dialogue in the workplace. Finally, chapter ten discusses briefly the state of public dialogue in politics and the possibility of cultivating a society of dialogists by means of a practical proposal for education. This proposal aims to nurture a citizenship with the reasoning ability, communication skills, and idealism necessary for a dialogic society.

Although each of the chapters emphasizes important individual aspects or uses of dialogue, you will discover that each contributes to the general understanding of dialogue as a whole.

In this work you will be introduced to principles for the dialogues that you will have in your own life. It is likely that you will have many questions about the ideas presented. A book, however, cannot enter into dialogue and answer questions about what it says. It is important, though, that you pursue your questions by considering them in your own mind and in dialogue with friends, because in the end, it is your own dialogues that must become the object of your study, a study that will allow you to establish your own principles and vision of this wonderful activity.

disagreement. Thus, dialogue unites us in a common goal despite our differences of opinion.

The act of entering into this structure called dialogue supersedes the content of the disagreement and forms the basis for a relationship. Conflicts appear at times unsolvable not necessarily because of the depth of disagreement, but because of the lack of a proper structure for the exploration of the disagreement. Simply put, the structure with which we seek to resolve a disagreement and seek understanding is as fundamental to the achievement of the goal of understanding as the discussion of the particulars involved.

There could be no more beneficial gain to our world than a deeper commitment and appreciation for genuine dialogue, for it is the power of dialogue to reveal truth and engender friendship among people. The classical principles and structure of dialogue have the potential to form the basis of a universal language of understanding that can unite humans. And there is certainly nothing that is more needed today. Our problems are no longer isolated in particular places; instead, our destiny as a species is necessarily intertwined. To the degree that we are able to transcend differences of culture, religion, race, sex, and economic class, we will be able to effectively work toward the solution of our common problems. To whatever extent these differences polarize us, we shall be blocked. Dialogue by itself will not solve our problems, but, inevitably, all our problems must be worked out through dialogue. Dialogue, therefore, is the necessary condition for solving problems.

In our individual lives dialogue is no less important. How much grief and anguish do we all experience because of our lack of ability in this area? There is no more important part of relationships, especially romantic ones, than communication. Naturally, dialogue is often the greatest challenge of a relationship. How many more marriages would succeed (or at least end more amicably) if the principles of genuine dialogue were understood and employed? Individuals also would be better prepared to choose the right spouse and avoid divorce altogether. How many families would function more harmoniously with a greater respect for genuine dialogue between parents and children? How much more well-being would exist in our home lives and future generations of children? And yet the situation is just the opposite. We yell and bicker amongst ourselves and within our families, playing out ancient family dramas and rarely reaching what we most desire—simple understanding.

In politics it is no different. Our leaders rival and contend with one another, and we, the public, grow more disillusioned. The journalists egg on the rivalry and contention like spectators at a wrestling match. We no longer trust our leaders or the idea that there is a shared concern for the country's common good—much less humanity's good. The same can be said for business as a whole. There no longer exists any trust between business leaders and workers, nor is there any trust that the leaders of industry share a concern for the good of the country, humanity, or the future of our planet—none of which comes as much of a surprise. America is based on the institutionalization of competition, and with competition, there is always rivalry and strife. This strife poses perhaps the greatest threat to human society and the life-sustaining environment of the planet.

The cultivation of a culture of dialogue is a means to challenge the unhindered rivalrous spirit that possesses our nation. Yet our country is far from having any appreciation of this. Our inability to communicate has become the source of a large part of our TV entertainment. This inability to communicate in a meaningful way has generated a plethora of so-called "talk shows" that enlist those who have strong beliefs on a topic of current interest, or who are in the midst of their personal dramas to come on national television with their antagonists to display anger and self-righteousness in public. There is no doubt that these shows can be entertaining. They showcase people filled with sincere emotions losing their tempers and saying outrageous things in the middle of discussions on outrageous topics. But what we need are more examples of successful communication.

Unfortunately, the political talk shows are no better. Although these programs are entertaining as well, it is disheartening to see how an opportunity for the meaningful exploration of an issue is lost to a concern for political success and ratings. And what is even sadder is that very often the most important issues facing our world have become the subjects of entertainment, rather than subjects of serious and careful consideration in the most rational and conscientious manner.

Unfortunately, these television shows have become a model for the discussion of ideas (as anyone who teaches high school or college has seen). But even the most sober discussion of ideas on television—because of the lack of a model for meaningful dialogue—presents a disparaging example for effective dialogue. For whenever a serious issue is taken on in the media, it is done in the following way: The issue is presented by a journalist. Then one expert gives his or her view of the matter. Usually, the argument sounds persuasive and the ideas well supported. Then a second expert is introduced. The second expert goes on to challenge the claims made by the first and introduces new information and evidence that appear to contradict in part or in whole the former's claims. The first expert challenges the claims of the second, and, in turn, the second rebuts the first. At this point a third expert may be introduced who stands somewhere in the middle between the first two. This format leads to confusion and can only make one wonder what the significance of being an expert is if all experts disagree. It also has created a social climate in which people have no trust in political or scientific leaders to work together to come to genuine answers to society's problems. Instead, it has instilled a common belief that everyone is just out to defend his or her own point of view.

It doesn't have to be this way. There exists a model of dialogue, a set of principles established for the meaningful exploration of ideas, a model established by ancient Greek philosophers whose goal was not debate and the war of words, but a genuine search for truth. We have inherited the principle of free speech and the free exchange of ideas from the ancient Greeks, but what we lack is their ideal of how we can best use this freedom for our benefit. By educating ourselves in this ancient ideal, we can regain this higher standard for ourselves, our society, and our leaders. For in both our individual lives and in our democracy, we have the freedom to let circumstances get worse or to seek to make them better. The goal of this book is to present this model of dialogue and show how it can help improve our lives and our world.

The Classical Model of Dialogue

Let us begin by first defining what a dialogue is. In essence, a dialogue is a discussion that focuses on a certain question or issue in which the participants join together to seek out the truth in a sincere and honest manner. The classical model of dialogue comes from Socrates' description of dialogue in Plato's *Meno*. The four parts of the model outline certain principles that we are all familiar with and that we utilize at times in our discussions with others. This model establishes formal guidelines and principles that people interested in dialogue can look toward as a standard for their own communication.

FOCUSED QUESTION

There are many forms of discussion, dialogue being one special form. The most common form of discussion is what we can call *conversation*. In a conversation people express different views on a range of subjects without concern for where the conversation goes and what twists and turns it may take. Often a conversation stays on a particular subject because it is considered important or interesting, but it doesn't necessarily have to. In order to have a dialogue, the speakers must make a shared and conscious decision to enter into dialogue, because a dialogue is a conscious endeavor. A dialogue begins with a specific question or issue for exploration and aims to remain on this path within a dialogue. Of course, within a dialogue there are times when an interesting side issue may arise. If the dialogists choose to follow the direction of the side issue, then they do so consciously, and this is termed a *digression*. (This issue is discussed further in chapter three.)

SEARCH FOR TRUTH

People join in dialogue in order to search for the truth. Therefore, the participants must trust that the truth of the issue exists. The opposite approach is that of the skeptic, who claims that the truth cannot be discovered. Whereas the skeptical approach closes us to the investigation and search, the truth-seeking approach makes us active and eager in our search and open to more possibilities. Even in the discussion of the most difficult issues, it is the desire for and trust in a genuine answer that must guide us in dialogue. In the search we do not abandon our own questions and concerns, but we do put aside our unsupported doubts. (This issue is discussed further in chapter four.)

FRIENDSHIP

We can enter into this discussion as friends or competitors. Competitors enter into dialogue to "win." Friends enter into dialogue because they seek the truth. When competitors enter into a discussion, it is no longer called a dialogue, but a debate; and in a debate, competitors no longer maintain the goal of truth, but instead use any means to win a war of words. In a friendly dialogue it is of no concern who is right or wrong; the only concern is for the truth. Dialogue demands the spirit of friendship because dialogue is a kind of relationship that calls for a spirit of care and concern, trust, understanding, and fairness from its participants. (This issue is discussed further in chapter five.)

FOLLOW THE LOGOS

As stated earlier, *logos* in the Greek language means "word" or "reason." We need this word in our language because it shows that we express our reasoning in words. Follow the logos means follow the word. The dialogist must follow the word, because the word is the expression of the speaker's mind and the very means of communication. For a dialogue to maintain its integrity, speakers and listeners must remain true to the words spoken. This goal requires that speakers try to express what they mean and listeners try to listen attentively and not interpret the words that are heard. Interpretation is the process whereby ones adds or subtracts ideas from what one reads or hears. In this process one changes the very meaning of what is said, and the integrity of the communication is lost. Following the logos is perhaps the greatest challenge of dialogue.

In order to follow the logos, the logos must be articulated and agreed upon. The participants must clearly express and decide how they define the key terms in the dialogue; they must also articulate and agree upon the principles of reasoning they appeal to when they make their arguments. When both key terms and principles are determined and articulated, the dialogists proceed together in the discussion. (This issue is discussed further in chapters three and four.)

The classical model of dialogue is as follows: The first part, the question, we call the *doorway* into dialogue; the second part, the goal, presents the goal of the journey—the *truth*; the third part introduces the way of the journeying—*friendship*; and the fourth part expresses the vehicle—the *logos*. This model functions as an ideal for our dialogues. By taking on this model in a conscious manner, we set a standard for our discussions, a standard that is agreed upon and clear to all the participants in the discussion. The standard then can function as a direction in and a course on which we want the dialogue to proceed; at the same time, we must remain aware that during this kind of journey it is likely we will often veer away from the set course, blown by the winds of emotion. By having a standard, however, there exists a compass and measure to which both of the dialogists may appeal in order to set the dialogue back on course with gentle reminders. All along, our ultimate aim is to discover the beauty and significance of this kind of journeying, traveling through reason and cultivating the steady wind of the logos to guide one's relationships, for it is ultimately the beauty of reason that drew the ancients to this form of communicating.

2 ORIGINS OF DIALOGUE IN ANCIENT GREECE

In ancient Greece the principles of dialogue reached the level of genuine art in a form called *dialectic* (the word *dialectic* comes from *dialogue* and means the way of dialogue), and the greatest master of this art was the Athenian philosopher Socrates. In his dialogues, Socrates displays the spontaneity of an improvisational musician, the wit of a stand-up comedian, the playfulness of a child, the focus and skill of a tai chi fighter, the intellectual genius of a chess master, and the beneficence of the truest friend. The focus of Socrates' dialogues is the exploration of the most significant questions of human life. What is the nature of this life? How ought a human being live? Many of the dialogues focus on a specific question: What is excellence? What is justice? What is love? In some dialogues Socrates shares his own vision of life, in addition to exploring the positions held by others. In all his dialogues Socrates follows the way of the logos, the path governed by the principles of dialectic.

Logos is the fundamental principle of ancient Greek culture, very similar to the Tao in Chinese culture. For both Chinese and Greek sages, the Tao, or the logos, is the indefinable power and source of all life. The goal of philosophy therefore is to strive to understand the nature of the logos so that one may live in harmony with it. The greatest expression of the Tao in Chinese thought is found in the

I Ching, and the most perfect understanding of the logos is presented in the dialogues of Plato, most especially his *Parmenides*.

The Greeks possessed a remarkably intellectual culture, but unlike society today, they did not divorce the intellectual life from the spiritual life. In other words, they were able to use their intellects to guide their spiritual growth and understanding. Consequently, when they discussed the nature of the logos in their reasonings, they did not reduce it to mere "logic," but voiced it rationally in such a way that it possessed genuine vitality. For example, one of the most fundamental of these rational principles states that *every multitude is preceded by a one*. This principle is clearly manifested in every aspect of nature. For example, according to physicists the universe was first a concentrated unity that exploded in the Big Bang, a "one" before a "many." Similarly, according to the theory of evolution, life began on our planet from one-celled animals and developed into much more complex life-forms.

A more vivid example, perhaps, is human life itself. Each human life begins its development in the mother's womb as a single cell called a zygote. This zygote possesses the complete genetic code in seedlike form for every aspect of the entire human organism. This cell therefore foresees, so to speak, the entire making of a human life, from the specific functioning of every particular cell and its role in bones, muscles, tissues, and organs to the color of one's eyes and the shape of one's fingernails. From this one cell there is a division into two and so on into greater complexity and multiplicity.

Greek theology (what today we call mythology) follows this same principle. Although there are many different gods, they are all born from the First God. And like the zygote, this First God contains in himself the nature of all the gods (who are the very powers of the cosmos) in the most primal way. In this respect the First God, sometimes called Zeus, possesses a vision of the totality of all that is and will be, but in a way that is not temporal, since the First God also exists beyond time. These examples, therefore, aim to illustrate how the Greeks could articulate rational principles that possessed a spiritual vitality. They sought to articulate these intellectual principles in order to see the logos more clearly in their lives, and the principles they discovered became the basis for the meaningful and fruitful exploration of ideas.

In dialogue, then, this same principle was used to direct inquiry. Socrates sought to discover the one belief that was central to an individual's thinking and was the source and cause of other beliefs, this one prior to the many. He often asked the question "What is excellence?" Socrates, however, would not accept any answer that appealed to particulars, such as "Excellence is being a great leader" or "Excellence is acquiring great wealth." Through this process of inquiry, he was able to help reveal how a belief could limit one's view of excellence and hinder one's personal development and spiritual growth. For example, one might believe that excellence is possible only for the ruling class or for men. By holding such a view, an individual would not see the universal nature of excellence as a unity that precedes the many different ways it is expressed in the world. Moreover, this prejudice would prevent an individual from fully appreciating and participating in the quality of excellence because he would not seek to cultivate the excellence of women and the populace of a city; therefore, he would lack excellence in his own life.

The ancient Greeks were in awe of reason, and it formed the basis of their culture and their ideal of education, or what they called *paideia*. The exploration of ideas and the pursuit of learning was not only the occupation of the young but also the most desired form of leisure. The interest among Greeks in knowledge and their desire for talent in speaking brought forth an entire class of professionals called Sophists. The Sophists were master knowers. Many Sophists claimed to have a command of mathematics, astronomy, politics, music, and the mastery of personal affairs. Although they sometimes differed in their emphasis, they all shared a common claim to mastery in the world of letters and public speaking, and all purported to be able to teach this skill to others.

Sophists traveled from city to city and vied with one another in regular contests of rhetorical jousting and Olympian contests of knowing. Those who were judged victorious gained a public renown that brought them a city's wealthiest students. The wealth they earned was astounding. The greatest of all Sophists was the famed Protagoras, who is said to have earned more in his lifetime than even Greece's most famed sculptor, Phideias, or more than ten other sculptors put together. The Sophist Gorgias was wealthy enough to dedicate a statue of himself in gold to the Oracle at Delphi.

Many of Plato's dialogues record accounts of Socrates' encounters with the Sophists. In these dialogues Socrates compelled the Sophists and their students to comply with the principles of dialectic. By appealing to the basic principles of reasoning and simple questioning, Socrates was able to draw out the contradictions in their positions, showing them to be false. The Athenian philosopher and dialectical watchdog challenged the Sophists and their false use of rhetoric for profit and power, proving himself the ultimate champion of these games. Yet he never attributed the victory to himself, but to Truth alone. For, as he said, it was easy to contradict Socrates but very difficult to contradict the truth.

The dialogues that Plato re-created in an art form are an imitation of a kind of event that was central to the culture of Greece. There were, in fact, many dialogic writers in the ancient Greek world, but Plato was the greatest. Enormous care was given to the preservation of his works by ancient scribes who had to meticulously copy each page every hundred years. Besides Plato's works, only one other ancient dialogue has come down to us through history. In contrast, we possess an entire lifetime of Plato's literary work, whole and intact.

A dialogue could be very brief or take an entire day and continue through the night. Plato also recorded dialogues that took place over successive days. What is most remarkable is that these dialogues could hold the attention of groups of people for the length of an entire day or longer. Plato's masterpiece the *Republic* is the record of a dialogue that would have taken a complete day to be held, and there is no mention of even one break through the entire work. What is perhaps more remarkable is that the *Republic* is presented as Socrates' recollection of the event to an unnamed person or group of people the following day. Two entire days of speaking! Yet this is consistent with Plato's portrayal of Socrates as a dialectical yogi.

Socrates is presented in Plato's dialogues as a unique individual with extraordinary powers. Most days Socrates spent in the public marketplace and civic center called the *agora*, engaging in dialogue with those he met. On occasion he spent his evenings out drinking with his friends at their banquets. Plato portrays him ending the evening by leaving his friends, who had all passed out, and going off to town to start his normal day at the public baths without even a wink of sleep. This kind of yogic energy is the goal of many yogic practices, and this sort of memory training was common in the ancient world. Francis Yates documents the history of the tradition in *The Art of Memory*. Indeed, a friend of mine and fellow philosopher practiced the Pythagorean memory training and was able to achieve such results. For two years he spent a number of hours each night recalling in a journal lectures and dialogues he had attended that day in as much detail as possible. With this training he was able to walk away from a discussion with the ability to recall it word for word.

Many of the introductions to Plato's dialogues also discuss how the recollection of the dialogue is presented. Whereas some are portrayed as occurring in the moment, others are recollections or recollections of other recollections that form a memory tradition. What these introductions reveal is that it was a matter of great concern from whom a recollection came, since a lack of understanding of the material or the influence of interpretation would undermine the integrity of the tradition. Thus, the Greek philosophical tradition emerged out of an oral tradition that was passed down not through writing, but through memory.

Ancient Greek is a language that possesses a natural mnemonic structure. Whereas in English it is considered poor style to repeat the same transitions or logical connectives (such as *then* or *therefore*), in Greek there are a series of words called *particles* that are relatively untranslatable but provided the Greek writer or speaker with a structure shared by all speakers within which he could organize his thoughts. The two most important particles are *men* and *de*. The nearest translations of them in English are "on the one hand" and "on the other hand." However, they have a much broader application and, as one can see, they are very simple to use, being one syllable rather than an entire phrase. The particles in Greek provide a nearly musical structure to the language, articulating introductions, supporting statements, contrasting statements, and introducing conclusions. Often one particle can carry the meaning of an entire sentence or paragraph without the need of even speaking it. Consequently, the listener can remember what was said using these particles to announce the different parts of a speech like the phrases and sections in a musical composition.

For one, the Greeks possessed leisure, which is the necessary condition for the development of an intellectual culture. And they had a boundless desire for learning and knowledge. Yet, like children, they engaged in this activity because they were filled with wonder and reveled in the exploration of ideas in a way that was both playful and joyful. In such a state there is, of course, no consciousness of time and therefore the possibility of profound growth. This kind of sustained attentiveness and focus is meditative. The center of this activity is the holding of a question or a puzzle, and this kind of meditative focus generates an energy that in Zen is called *joriki*. It is a state in which the mind is both calm and profoundly clear and provides the condition for insight; when that kind of insight occurs, it is energizing. One can see that being a part of the audience to a dialogue is an opportunity to engage in an intellectual and meditative activity that is cathartic and energizing, and a source of insight, learning, and growth.

The Greek culture of dialogue and reason grew out of the practice of council that was used by the kings of the Greek world in the Homeric age (approximately 1200 B.C.E.). In Homer's great epic, the *Iliad*, the kings of many different Greek cities and lands joined together to help Menelaos, the king of Sparta, regain his wife, Helen, who had gone off with the Trojan prince, Paris. These kings came together under the leadership of Menelaos's brother, Agamemnon, the marshall of the entire Greek army. These kings regularly joined together in council to consider the best plan to achieve their ends. The Greek word for council is *voule* and is sometimes also translated as "will" (related to *volition* and the French *vouloir*, or "to want").

The main theme of the *Iliad* is the conflict between the Greeks' greatest warrior, Achilles, and the commander of the army, Agamemnon. Because of his anger, Achilles quits the battle, and the tide of the war turns and threatens to destroy the Greek army. Thus, in the opening of the *Iliad*, the anger of Achilles and the destruction it caused the Greek army are said by Homer, the Muse-inspired poet, to be "the will [voule] of Zeus." In Greek theology the gods will only what is good. Therefore, the will of Zeus is what he thought to be best. It then becomes the goal of wisdom and intelligence to discover why the anger of Achilles, or any other tragic event, can serve an ultimately good end.

In today's world, intelligence is often identified by a quantifiable measure of one's ability to do practical calculation in logic or math. This is a far cry from the Greek idea of intelligence and wisdom, called *phronesis*. Phronesis is the kind of wisdom that emerges from a clear mind. With phronesis one has the ability to penetrate deeply into the heart of an issue to grasp which path will lead an individual or group toward a desired end, that is, an end or goal whose achievement will bring benefit. Often this is a matter of weighing out the pros and cons of different possible approaches to a situation. However, this wisdom called phronesis goes further. It is a power that enables one also to delve more deeply into an issue and reveal possibilities that were not clearly apparent to others but, when revealed, are recognized as the best and clearest path to the desired end.

In council, the Homeric kings joined together to hear one another express their minds and what they saw as best—that is, what their minds willed to be done. Although one could sometimes use rhetoric to make an idea appear best, the ultimate standard or judge of the wisdom of one's council was a measure that was indisputable—the outcome of taking the particular course of action that the council willed. In this way, the ancient heroes earned their reputations for their ability or lack of ability to provide good counsel. In the ancient world Odysseus was renowned for his wisdom and good counsel. Thus he was said to be the beloved of Athena, the goddess of wisdom and courage, who was born out of the head (that is, the mind) of her father, Zeus, fully dressed for battle. And so it was Odysseus who proposed to the other Greeks that they build the Trojan horse and in this way end the siege of Troy's great walled citadel through cleverness, after ten years of their warcraft had failed.

Homer's great epic, though, is not an account of the Trojan War as a whole. The entire drama of the poem takes place within a few days in the last year of the war and ends before the capture of Troy. Instead, it is the story of the anger of the Greek warrior Achilles. Achilles withdraws from the battle after a conflict with Agamemnon, pulls out the troops under his command, and threatens to leave Troy for his homeland in Myrmidon. The consequences for the Greeks are devastating.

Finally recognizing the dire nature of the situation, Agamemnon and the Greek kings hold a council to determine what to do. They decide to send a group of emissaries to Achilles to try to persuade him to give up his anger and return to the battle. The emissaries present to Achilles Agamemnon's offer of the most magnificent fortune and treasures. They also speak to him in the wisest of words. In his heart Achilles himself wants these honors and desires to return to the battle so that he can earn immortal fame, but still he rejects their pleas, for he is in the grip of an anger that is "sweeter than slow-dripping honey." Thus, at the center of the drama of the *Iliad* is the crisis that ensues when reason appears to have no persuasive power over an individual in the midst of such crisis; it goes on to unfold the tragic consequences for this individual and for those around him. This is the essence of the Greek idea of tragedy.

Tragedy occurs when one is blocked from doing what is most beneficial for oneself and one's friends or community. The Greek tragedians expressed with genius the dynamics of this drama in various ways, and what they identified as the root and source of this tragic block is a certain kind of belief—the belief that one knows what is good and true when in reality it is just the opposite. *Thus, the condition of tragedy is the belief that one thinks one knows, when one really does not know.* In the case of Achilles, he thought it was best to hold on to his anger, but in the end it cost him that which he most loved, the life of his best friend, Patroclus. Although the tragedians displayed this drama, they did not offer a solution or therapy for the condition that they identified as plaguing mankind. Instead, they portrayed to what great and awful depths one must fall in order to awaken from folly and ignorance. This state of folly was attributed to the power of Ate, the goddess who misleads men. The tragedians displayed the archetypes of human ignorance as vividly as possible so that individuals could see the nature of such folly more clearly and thus attempt to avoid it.

The ancient philosophers, however, and Socrates most specifically, did introduce a means to deal with the problem of human ignorance. Socrates brought to birth an art that aims to free the human being from the power and spell of Ate. Indeed, Socrates devoted his life to questioning himself and others concerning this very issue at the heart of human tragedy. Through questioning he constantly sought to discover whether he himself and the people around him truly were in a state of knowing or were merely *thinking* they knew, when in truth they did not know. By this method of questioning, Socrates sought to bring forth those false beliefs that were the root of ignorance. He therefore called his art a kind of midwifery, since it sought to help in the delivery of beliefs. He then went on to say that his art surpassed ordinary midwifery since philosophical midwives have the responsibility of judging the truth or falsity of the beliefs that are brought to birth.

Plato has Socrates present an account of himself and his art in a dialogue called the *Theaetetus*. In this dialogue, Socrates asks a young student named Theaetetus if he is able to give an account of the unity that embraces the many different kinds of knowledge.

Socrates: Come now, you just lead the way most excellently—follow your answer about the roots, and just as you grasped the many in one form, try now in the same way also to grasp the many kinds of knowledge in one statement.

Theaetetus: Know well, Socrates, I often do attempt to look for this very thing when I hear the questions that people carry away from their encounters with you. But I am not able to persuade myself that what I say is sufficient, nor am I able to find anyone else who can answer in the way you say these questions must be answered. And yet I cannot free myself from this desire to find out.

Socrates: Theaetetus, my friend, this is because you are in the throes of labor, for you are not empty—you are pregnant.

Theaetetus: I don't know about that. I am simply telling you what I've been experiencing.

Socrates: Have you not heard, my foolish boy, that I am the son of a most noble and stately midwife, Phaenarete?

Theaetetus: I have heard that.

Socrates: And have you heard this, that I practice the same art?

Theaetetus: No, I've never heard that.

Socrates: Know well that this is true. But don't give me away to everyone else in the city. For it has escaped their notice, my friend, that I possess this same art. And since they don't know it, they don't say anything about it when they speak about me. Instead, they say I am strange and that I make others become puzzled and at a loss. Have you heard that about me?

Theaetetus: Oh, yes.

Socrates: Shall I tell you the reason for my reputation?

Theaetetus: Of course!

Socrates: Keep in mind the midwives' art as it is as a whole, and you will easily learn what I am willing to share with you. For you know, I suppose, that no woman who is still able to become pregnant and conceive practices midwifery for another; they practice only when they reach the point when they are no longer able to conceive.

Theaetetus: Of course.

Socrates: They say Artemis is responsible for this; since she is a virgin goddess, she was allotted childbirth as her portion. But she did not give the art of midwifery to women who are unable to bear children because human nature is too weak to gain an art of which it has no experience. Instead, she assigned it to those who are unable to conceive on account of their age and thereby honored their likeness to herself.

21

Theaetetus: That is likely.

Socrates: And is this also likely and necessary, that the midwives can distinguish better than any others who is pregnant and who is not?

Theaetetus: Certainly.

Socrates: And this, too, that when they administer drugs or chant incantations, the midwives are able to rouse the throes of labor or soften them, that is, when they will it necessary? And aren't they also able to make those who have difficulty conceiving conceive? And don't they decide when the birth is premature, and if it appears to them necessary to perform an abortion, they do so?

Theaetetus: These things are true

Socrates: Have you then also perceived this about them, that midwives possess the most gifted minds for matchmaking, since they are perfectly wise in discerning with what kind of man it is necessary for a certain kind of woman to join in intercourse so as to conceive the most excellent children?

Theaetetus: No, I did not know that.

Socrates: Know this, too, that they think more highly of this than their ability in cutting the umbilical cord. For consider this. Do you suppose it is the same art that cares for and gathers in the harvest of the fruits of the earth, on the one hand, and yet a different art that discerns what kind of soil and what kind of plant and seed it is necessary to sow?

Theaetetus: No, the same.

Socrates: In respect to women, my friend, do you suppose there is one art for mating and yet another for the harvest?

Theaetetus: That's not likely at all.

Socrates: But there is an unjust way of bringing men and women together that lacks art, called *pandering*, and it is on this account that midwives do not employ their art to mindfully arrange relationships, for they are righteous women and fear being accused of pandering. And yet the true midwives are the only ones who possess the mind for matchmaking.

Theaetetus: It seems so.

Socrates: The art of the midwives is very great; nonetheless, it falls short of what I do. For women do not give birth to images sometimes and true offspring at other times. It is not easy to make this

22

kind of distinction. But if midwives were to judge the true
and the false, it would be their greatest and noblest deed.
Don't you think so?

Theaetetus: Yes, I do.

Socrates: All that belongs to these midwives also belongs to my
art of midwifery, but my art does differ in these respects. I
practice midwifery on men and not women, and I examine
the offspring of their souls and not their bodies. But the
greatest part of my art is to be able to test in every way
whether the thought of a youth that is born to light is an image and falsehood or a genuine offspring and true. And there
is also this that I share with the midwives. I am childless in
wisdom, and what the many reproach me with is true. I ask
others questions, but I do not answer at all myself about anything because I have no wisdom. The reason for this is as follows. The God requires me to be a midwife, and so he prevented me from giving birth. I am therefore not at all a wise
man, nor does there exist any kind of enlightened discovery
in me born as an offspring from my soul. And although those
who associate with me at first appear sometimes very ignorant, all of them after continuing in this relationship with me,
that is, those with whom the God allows me to relate, make
marvelous growth, as they themselves and their friends recognize. And it is clear that they are never learning anything from
me, but that they discover and bring forth many beautiful
learnings by themselves and from themselves.

And, in truth, both the God and myself are responsible
for the delivery. And here is the proof. Many who are ignorant of this have attributed the delivery of these beautiful
learnings to themselves and have scorned me and have persuaded themselves to leave sooner than was needed. By leaving they have aborted their remaining offspring on account
of their bad relations, and through their bad nurturing they
have also killed the offspring delivered by me. They have
made falsehood and images more important than truth and
so, in the end, have shown themselves ignorant to themselves
and to others. One of these is Lysimachus's son, Aristeides,

and there have also been many others. When they come back again in need of the relationship with me and do remarkable things to get it, sometimes my daimon comes and prevents me from relating to them. But at other times it allows it, and again these people continue their growth. And, of course, the ones who associate with me have the same experience in giving birth. They go through the throes of labor and become filled with puzzlement both night and day, much more than those whom the God blocks me from associating with. My art is able to both rouse and cease the throes of labor, and those who are pregnant are affected accordingly.

Sometimes, though, Theaetetus, there are some who do not appear to me to be pregnant at all, and since I know that they are in no need of my art, in a very kindly manner, I arrange a relationship for them. With the help of the God, I most satisfactorily place them in relationships that I believe are likely to benefit them. Many of these people I have given to Prodicus as students, and many to other wise and divine-sounding men. Now, I have explained this at length to you, my beautiful boy, for this reason. I suspect that you are in the throes of labor with something and in need of giving birth to it, as, indeed, you yourself suppose. Bring yourself to me as to the midwife's son and to my maieutic art, and the questions I ask eagerly answer however you are able. And when, in my examination of what you say, I lead to birth an image and untruth and I lift it away from under you and discard it, don't be savagely angry, like a mother protecting her firstborn. For there have been many already, oh marvelous youth, who were so angry at me that they were altogether prepared to bite me when I took away some foolishness from them. And they did not think that I did this because of my concern for them, since they were far from knowing that no god has bad intent toward man, nor do I perform this function with any bad intent. But it is the law of my very nature never to yield to falsehood nor to hide the truth. And so now, once again, from the beginning, Theaetetus, what after all is knowledge? Try to say. Do not ever say you are not able, for when the God wishes and gives you courage, you will be able.*

---

* Translation by Robert Apatow.

Socrates practiced his art of midwifery through dialogue with others. The dialogues of Plato show him practicing this art and testing the beliefs and knowledge that others claim to have. This philosophical art is the highest use of the principles of dialogue. Thus, it was very important for Socrates and other philosophers to express very clear principles about how dialogues ought to proceed. The model of dialogue that will be presented in this book is shared by the philosophical midwife, but the midwife's art goes beyond it. Those who wish to seek out these principles must try to master the dialogues of Plato and discover what Socrates is and how he functions. We shall never know who the historical Socrates really was. Plato presents him as the ideal philosopher. Socrates dedicated his life to the love of wisdom and truth. For the ancients, nothing surpassed wisdom and truth in beauty; thus, the philosopher was also called a lover of beauty. From his youth, Socrates was enamored of this path in life and is presented as a student with two of the greatest figures in philosophy, Parmenides, the master dialectician, and Diotima, a seer and priestess who guided the young Socrates in the mysteries of love.

Socrates had a rich background in the Wisdom tradition of the ancient Hellenes and became an accomplished yogi and master of dialectic himself. In a famous passage from Plato's *Symposium*, Socrates is said to have been a fierce warrior and one who was not troubled by even the coldest weather. His colleague in the Greek army gives an account of him walking barefoot in the snow. These same kinds of feats are common among the great yogis of Tibet, who are able to generate the internal heat called *thumos* (curiously, the Tibetan word is the Greek word for spirit or energy that Plato uses in the *Republic*). He also tells of how Socrates stood in meditation from one dawn to the next without moving. In the Greek world, such a master yogi did not isolate himself from society. Socrates was not a priest or a monk. He was a stone-carver, a soldier, and a husband and father, who on the day he was put to death at the age of seventy-two is pictured holding his baby son on his knee. Thus, this great yogi lived a worldly life. In the Greek world the challenge was to gain wisdom and bring it into society in a way that could benefit one's fellow human being.

Socrates, however, never engaged in politics, because he was turned away from this activity by a spiritual guide that he called a *daimon*—literally a spirit or demigod. In the *Apology*, he explains that this daimon never told him what to do but would guide him away from what he should not do. Nonetheless, Socrates considered himself the only true statesman in Athens, because he sought to question his fellow citizens on the way they lived and compelled them to account for themselves. In this way, he sought to direct them away from the concern for wealth and power to a concern for living with genuine excellence.

Socrates is what is called a *jnani yogin*, a yogi whose practice is the exercise of the mind, and he practices his yoga in dialogues with others. In these dialogues he is an archetype and ideal for us to look to today. As he reports in *Theaetetus*, Socrates says that he is not wise and thus can function most ideally as a midwife. He is freed from any opinions or prejudices that may block him from understanding what is being said. Moreover, he seeks to benefit others through this practice, so that truth will be revealed, showing the deepest concern for others' well-being. Socrates does not take on a false role as a knower or wise man to foster his self-image. In the Greek view of art, as I mentioned earlier, one practices the art not for one's own benefit but for the benefit of the subject who is in need of the art. For example, the doctor does not practice his art of medicine for his own benefit, but for the benefit of the patient. According to the principles of the medical profession, the doctor is paid for his time and not for his knowledge. Socrates, however, never requested fees for his company, but always entered into dialogue out of pure friendship and consequently lived a life of relative poverty.

Socrates practiced dialogue in the spirit of friendship; yet when he encountered hostility, he was able to keep his cool, hold his own, and bring to bear a manner of sincerity and directness that enabled the dialogue to continue, despite the aggressiveness of his interlocutor. Many in Athens, though, were quite suspicious of Socrates and the kind of life he led. In fact, Socrates reports that there was a long-standing prejudice against philosophers in his day. Many of the

Athenian citizens were not happy with Socrates after encountering him in dialogue, since they were often shown to think that they knew when they really did not. Consequently, some of the more powerful citizens brought Socrates to trial and charged him with corrupting the youth, not believing in the city's gods, and introducing new and strange divinities into the city. Socrates was found guilty and put to death. At the end of the dialogue that narrates Socrates' last day, one of his friends says, "This was the end of our comrade, a man, as it appears to me, of all those we had known in that time, the noblest and the wisest and the most just."

As a master of the art of dialogue, Socrates embodies the ideals and principles of his art in his very life. The life and character that Plato presents to us represent an ideal that we could all benefit from studying. The examination of Socrates' life, though, is essential for those who seek to practice the principles of dialogue, for he provides a model for how we may try to function in our discussions with others.

3 RULES AND PRINCIPLES FOR DIALOGUE

Dialogue As a Form of Play

The philosophical dialogues of ancient Greece were considered a form of leisure in that remarkable culture, and as an activity of leisure they were approached as a type of play, though admittedly a highly intellectual type of play. In contemporary life we most often seek out the path of dialogue to explore difficult and serious issues in our lives, relationships, and work. And yet, the very activity of dialogue can be seen as a certain kind of play, and by putting the activity in this perspective we are in a better position to most fully enjoy the benefits of fruitful and insightful dialogues.

In the book *Homo Ludens: A Study of the Play Element in Culture,* Johan Huizinga explores a variety of human cultural activities that emerged as kinds of play. It is Huizinga's thesis that the human being is distinguished from other animals not simply by his capacity for thought but also for play, and so can be called not only *Homo sapiens,* but also *Homo ludens,* man the player. In this book he looks specifically at language, poetry, art, knowing, law, war, and philosophy. Huizinga explains that play "is a free activity standing quite consciously outside 'ordinary' life as being 'not serious,' but at the same time absorbing the player intensely and utterly. It is an activity connected with no material interest, and no profit can be gained by it. It proceeds within its own proper boundaries of time and space according to fixed rules and in an orderly manner. It promotes the formation of social groupings."*

In a culture that very strictly delineates work from play, the serious from the not serious, it sounds surprising to hear things like law or war labeled as play. Yet, at the same time, we all know that many of the most successful people engaged in these activities consider them to be games they play. They can be called games because, like the games of children, they have certain rules and boundaries located in time and space and absorb the players "intensely and utterly." They also have intrinsic value and are therefore worth doing for their own sake. A dialogue is a kind of play, but a higher kind of play, for it aims at truth. In dialogue, as in other kinds of play, we step outside ordinary life to reflect on and discuss an issue of concern within our lives. Dialogue demands a kind of leisure from our everyday affairs, at which time we can step out into what Huizinga calls a "temporary sphere of activity with a disposition all of its own."

There are many activities that have this kind of quality. A court proceeding, a political debate, and a play all take place within certain boundaries that separate these activities from ordinary life. This marking off establishes that there is a need for a special focus to exist. In order to create this focus, there must be agreement among the participants and listeners in regard to the rules, time, and setting of the activity. Without these boundaries, such focus cannot be established. In the same way, a dialogue must also be given a life of its own by marking off a "temporary sphere" in which the activity can take place.

Like other forms of play, dialogue possesses its own proper disposition or quality, which is characterized by the flow of the logos. Of all the activities that exist, a good dialogue has as much power as any to absorb our interest. Stan Getz, the great tenor saxophonist,

---

*Johan Huizinga, *Homo Ludens: A Study of the Play Element in Culture* (Boston: Beacon Press, 1955), p. 130.

said that no art form besides jazz can give the satisfaction of spontaneous interaction, except for conversation. "A good quartet, listening closely to each other, is like good conversation among friends interacting to each other's ideas." He is, of course, referring to a looser form of discussion, but the point is the same. Within dialogue there is a life and a flow that are dynamic and in which we are able to participate.

Forms of play gain their existence by their setting and also by their rules. In music, for example, there must exist rhythm and harmony to unite the different players. Even in the improvisation of jazz, a soloist must play within the limits set by the meter and chord progression governing the tune. So also dialogue must take place within certain guidelines. Once established, this structure becomes the ground for bringing people together toward the common goal of understanding.

The Rules of the Game

Let us begin by establishing the boundaries of this activity called dialogue. Although there are many kinds of discussion, dialogue is one special form. The most common form of discussion is what we call *conversation*. In a conversation people express different views on a range of subjects without concern for where the conversation goes and what twists and turns it takes. Often a conversation will stay on a particular subject because it is considered important or interesting, but it doesn't necessarily have to have such boundaries. In order to have a dialogue, though, the speakers must make a shared and conscious decision to enter into dialogue, because it is a conscious endeavor based on a standard for meaningful communication.

A dialogue begins with a specific question or issue for exploration and aims to remain on this path. It is important to make the question or issue as specific as possible so that the dialogue can remain focused. By establishing the topic of the dialogue, the players can work together to keep the discussion on track. When a discussion stays on track, it is more likely to be fruitful in helping the participants better understand each other and the issue, much more so than if the discussion goes off randomly in many directions. When dialogists commit to a focused question, they will be able to judge at the end of the dialogue how far they have come toward reaching their goal and also what remains to be discussed in further meetings.

Within most dialogues, of course, there will be many interesting side issues that arise. The model of dialogue we are outlining here does not exclude the exploration of these issues, for to do so would be an injustice to the flow of the logos; an exploration into a side issue may sometimes be essential to the dialogue as a whole. If the dialogists choose to follow the direction of the side issue, they must do so deliberately and this is called a *digression*. The caveat of digressions is that when they are made, the dialogists must maintain their intent to return to the original question. In some cases, however, the parties may find that the digression is more important than the subject of the dialogue and may choose to abandon the topic of the dialogue in favor of the digression. In this case the digression becomes the new topic of dialogue. That is the choice of the dialogists. Bear in mind, though, that if the dialogue was important enough to start in the first place, it is likely that it will be considered important to set aside another time for the original discussion. If these digressions repeatedly take the dialogists away from their goal, it would be important for them to maintain discipline and finish the original dialogue or to consider why they are having difficulty staying with the original topic.

The Players

Now that we have established the boundaries for this kind of play, let us consider the specific roles that the players must take on and the rules, or guidelines, they must follow. First let us consider the roles. The two primary roles are that of the questioner and answerer. The questioner is usually the person who initially raises the question, but a dialogue does not have to proceed that way. Either party may choose to be the questioner or answerer. But what is essential is that each player is offered the opportunity to play both roles.

Socrates had the reputation in Athens for being the person who asked all the questions and never gave any answers, but that is not the truth of the matter. The truth is that Socrates was always willing to answer. Often though, his answer was very brief because he would readily admit that he didn't know, which often surprised his interlocutor, who didn't know how to continue the dialogue. And in the meantime, Socrates would quickly take over the role of questioner; by the time that he had finished questioning the other, the answerer was left in such a state of puzzlement that he gave up the opportunity to play questioner.

The questioner takes the responsibility of directing the dialogue. In order to do this, she must appreciate the question at issue and have in mind a direction for the inquiry to take. Moreover, she must be able to deal with the answerer's words and raise appropriate questions that move the dialogue in a meaningful direction. Some may suppose that this demands great knowledge, but according to Socrates it does not. What it requires is that the questioner genuinely seeks to understand the other person's position and ask the natural questions that emerge from the answers given.

One of the keys to accomplishing this is not to take anything for granted. Very often in discussions people do not complete their sentences or thoughts, and the listener goes on to assume she understands what the speaker intends to say. The danger here is that we add our own ideas to the speaker's and as a result may miss completely the speaker's intention. Therefore, it is essential that the questioner demand that the answerer fully complete her thoughts. When these thoughts are not completely clear, the questioner must invite the answerer to elucidate. The ultimate goal of the questioner is to draw out fully the position that the answerer is holding and then to explore its implications. In other words, the questioner assumes the answerer's position is true and then considers what things follow from it. Once this is done, the questioner and answerer must look at the picture they have made of the position and its implications and decide if it makes sense and whether it is true or false.

We all regularly enter into these kinds of explorations in a variety of ways. Every time we consider whether to make a significant purchase of a car, or a stereo, or even a product at the supermarket, we go through a similar sort of dialogue in our minds or with others. In this respect, we all understand the process of dialogue and are able to engage in it. At the same time, however, there is a background and training that can help improve one's ability to enter into dialogue. (This topic is discussed further in this chapter and in Appendix I.)

As mentioned earlier, the prefix *dia* in the word *dialogue* is from the Greek word for "through" and not the Greek word *duo,* which means "two." Dialogue is not the opposite of monologue. A dialogue is an exploration that can be shared by two or more people. A single individual, of course, may also wish to have a dialogue with him- or herself, and that can be a very effective way of exploring ideas as well. In order to do that, the individual plays out the roles of both questioner and answerer. (Chapter Seven, *The Inner Dialogue,* explores this topic further.) Most dialogues, though, are held between two people who each take on the two primary roles.

It is possible for two or more people to play each of the roles. This makes the dialogue much more challenging, because the possibility of getting sidetracked or of misunderstanding increases exponentially with the addition of each player. But, the addition of more players can have the potential to add more insight and integrity to the dialogue. The key, as always, is the ability of the players to work together to preserve the integrity of the logos, that is, the flow of reasoning in the dialogue and attention to the words and positions being explored. This demands a high level of objectivity from the participants.

The other participant (or participants) in a dialogue is the audience. Most often a dialogue takes place before only a small number of people, but it is also possible for it to take place within a large room. With television and satellite broadcasting, a dialogue could be conducted before the entire world. The role of the audience is to follow the dialogue as best it can. It is essential for the audience to preserve its role and not to interfere and interrupt the dialogue, for once audience members enter a dialogue, the focus is disrupted. In classical dialogue there is an implicit agreement on the part of participants to work together; all that is developed in the dialogue is based on this explicit agreement. When a new party enters, he adds a voice that has not participated in the development of the dialogue, nor in these implicit and explicit agreements.

There are, however, active roles that an audience can play. Traditionally, it is often the responsibility of the audience to help preserve the correct memory of the dialogue and to pass the recollection on to those who may wish to learn about it. An audience member or members can also play the role of arbiters in a disagreement about the course of the dialogue and upon request can intervene to give an account of the correct recollection of the dialogue. Audience members can also be asked to function as judges who are requested to help maintain objectivity in the dialogue and to assist the players to remain on their topic.

Reasoning and Understanding

Although one need not have any background in philosophy or logic to be a questioner, a familiarity with the basic models of reasoning is certainly helpful. It is essential for anyone who enters into dialogue and the communication of ideas to have a clear model of what understanding is and what it is not. This model then becomes a standard with which we can judge whether we or another understands an issue. With this standard we can judge whether we are in a position to explain something to another and whether we are clearly understanding another. Without a model and means to judge, this is impossible. The clearest and best model of reasoning is found in Euclid's *Elements of Geometry*. The study of Euclid's treatise was considered the foundation of *all* education—not merely for its introduction to the field of geometry, but also because it introduces the student to what clear reasoning truly is. For two thousand years, Euclid's approach to the presentation of ideas was the model used by scientists and philosophers, such as Isaac Newton, Spinoza, and Proclus.

In Appendix I, a brief introduction to the structure Euclid employs in his classic work is presented. The reader will discover that Euclid's approach is one that can be applied to any presentation of ideas in written or oral form. Euclid establishes three bases to his system of geometry: a set of *definitions* of the geometrical objects he discusses (e.g., a point is that which has no part); a set of *postulates*, which are procedures and principles specific to his subject, that is, geometry (e.g., how to draw a straight line from any point to any point); a set of *common notions*, or principles of reasoning common to all subjects of knowledge (e.g., things equal to the same thing are equal to one another).

All of the reasoning in his work is based upon his definitions, postulates, and common notions. In most contemporary mathematics and logic, the postulates and common notions are grouped together as the *axioms* of a system, literally, the starting points, though Euclid distinguishes those axioms that are specific to the subject being discussed (postulates) and those that are common to all subjects (common notions). Most people today do not make this distinction, however, you may find it helpful to do so in some dialogues.

Euclid's goal is to present a formal system. The way of dialogue is much more informal, but the same steps must be followed. It is essential for dialogists to make sure that they define and agree upon the definitions of the key terms in a dialogue. Second, as dialogists proceed to draw out the key steps in their reasoning on a subject, they must explain the basis for their reasoning. In other words, they must make clear why it is reasonable to move from one point to the next.

The problem in most discussions and debates is that neither party takes the time to establish an agreement upon the key terms and principles. In such discussions the participants rarely ever gain a better understanding of the issue or each other's positions. A good example of this kind of difficulty is evident in the debate over abortion rights. Central to this controversial issue is the question of how one defines the life that is growing within the mother's womb. The way one names and defines this life will determine many important implications. For example, if one says that the fetus is a person, it follows according to the traditional ethical and legal understanding of personhood that this person possesses certain rights. However, if one denies that it is a person, then the fetus does not possess these rights.

When we say that people are talking past one another, it usually expresses the idea that they are reasoning according to definitions and principles that have not been agreed upon. This is not a dialogue, but a kind of debate. Dialogue means that the participants move together step by step based on agreement or shared questions. When dialogists discover there is disagreement about definitions or principles, this disagreement must become the subject of the dialogue. In our example concerning the abortion issue, dialogists must first discuss the definition and status of the growing life before moving on to the question of a woman's right to abortion.

When dialogists reach an impasse in these kinds of difficult questions, there is a means to continue dialogue without complete agreement. To continue with our example, instead of coming to an agreed definition of the growing life, the dialogists may choose *the method of hypothesis.* In this method the dialogue continues on the basis of a hypothetical definition (or principle). The speakers can agree to consider what follows if the growing life is defined as a person, on the one hand, and a potential person, on the other hand. (Some people hold the position that there is a certain time when the fetus gains the rights of personhood, and, thus, they say that the growing life is a potential person.) In this way the dialogists can continue to explore the issue in an objective way and gain a fuller appreciation of the various ways it can be approached and about how it is reasoned. Moreover, in the course of a hypothetical dialogue, there is always the chance of gaining further insight about the original disagreement. In this way of proceeding, since the dialogue is based on different hypotheses, neither participant is committed to the conclusions reached.

All arguments are, in a certain respect, hypothetical, because they rest upon definitions and axioms that constitute the foundation of the argument. (An argument is the formal term for a set of reasonings leading to a conclusion.) The strength of any conclusion, therefore, is always dependent upon the strength of this foundation; what is most interesting is that this foundation always remains unproved. Definitions and principles are never proved themselves. Instead, they are the basis for the proof of other things. Euclid's first geometrical argument, for example, rests upon the definition that a triangle is a plane figure contained by three sides. Euclid does not offer any proof of this. He asks the reader to accept it as reasonable and self-evident. In the same way, he asks the reader to accept the common notion that things equal to the same things are also equal to one another. There can be no proof of such a principle, since it merely expresses what is implicit in the meaning of the idea of equality. Definitions and principles may be reasonable and appear self-evident, but none has any real proof to support them. In this respect, no argument can ever lead to certainty. Instead, arguments are a means to articulate what reasonably follows from what we consider to be true in our thinking and experience. (We shall further explore the issue of truth in the next chapter.)

Since all arguments depend upon their foundations, it is essential in a dialogue to attempt to state clearly and precisely what the definitions and principles of reasoning are. For if you assume starting points that your dialogic partner does not accept, there no longer exists a genuine dialogue. You then reason alone. You may establish a conclusion, but that conclusion will not be acceptable to the other party. The goal of dialogue is to proceed together step by step, and this is accomplished by articulating and agreeing upon the definitions of key terms and principles.

What you will discover if you attempt this approach is that it demands much more patience, time, and attention; however, such preparation will yield its results in the significance of the discussion. This model of reasoning can be likened to the building of a house. The definitions and principles (the starting points of a discussion) are like the foundation of the house, the steps in reasoning are like the stairway, and the steps along the stairway of reasoning lead one to a conclusion, which can be compared to the second floor. Of course, the whole building is only as solid as the foundation it is built upon.

Mathematics is an ideal model of understanding, because to study mathematics requires that we pay careful attention to every detail and step along the way in order to fully understand the material. You can't rush through mathematical reasoning, though you can pretend that you understand when you don't. The study of something like geometry demands that we take on a very different kind of rhythm to our reasoning. It is not fast paced and brief; it must be relaxed and complete.

In one of my courses my students worked through the first book of Euclid's *Elements*. Each day we took one or two propositions, and a student would read it aloud. After a student read a few sentences, I asked him, "Are you following what you are reading?" And the answer was always "No." I explained to the students that one of the main goals in studying Euclid's work is to practice understanding; therefore, the student reading aloud should read at a pace that allowed both her and the other students in the class the time to look back and forth at the diagram and put together the reasoning in their minds. And yet, despite these directions, which were repeated quite often, the students continued reading at a pace that prevented them from following the material. No doubt this is symptomatic of our society. We are bombarded with so much information and at such a fast pace that often we are unable to really understand anything.

A dialogue about an important issue between two or more people must be very different. It cannot proceed like sound bites from the evening news or the rush of slogans in fifteen-second commercials, or even the flow of words in a movie or popular novel. In a dialogue, players must consider every word carefully and mindfully, so that each player can understand the points that the other makes and how they each reason from point to point. An excellent example of an argument that articulates its principles can be found in Plato's dialogue *Crito*. This dialogue takes place in Socrates' jail cell the day before his execution. Socrates' friend Crito comes early that morning to try to persuade Socrates to escape. Crito attempts to convince

Socrates by appealing to his emotions. He tells Socrates that he is betraying his sons, doing to himself what his enemies wish, and being a coward. Socrates responds in a most beautiful fashion:

Socrates: Crito, my friend, your eagerness to persuade me is very admirable, if there is something right in it, but if not, the greater your argument the more difficult it will be for me to hold to the truth. Therefore, we must examine whether this thing ought to be done or not. For I am the sort of man, not only now but always, who is persuaded by nothing other than the reasoning which upon reflection seems best to me. These principles which I have expressed in the past I am not able to throw away now that this fortune has come to me, but I honor and venerate them as I did before.

Socrates will not do what his friend urges him to do even if his life is at stake. Instead, he will abide by his principle to act according to what appears to him most reasonable in each situation.

Socrates: Shall we say we must not willingly act unjustly in any way? Or may we commit some unjust acts, but not others? Or shall we say, as we have agreed many times in the past, that it is never right or good to act unjustly . . . ?

Crito: We shall say so.

Socrates: Then we ought not act unjustly in any way?

Crito: We ought not.

Socrates: Neither, then, ought we respond unjustly even after suffering injustice, as the many believe it is right to do, since we must never act unjustly?

Crito: It seems not.

Socrates: Then what about this? Ought we do wrong, Crito, or not?

Crito: We ought not, I suppose, Socrates.

Socrates: What about this? Is it just, as the many say, to do wrong in return after suffering a wrong, or is it not just?

Crito: It is not just at all.

Socrates: Doing wrong to people, I suppose, is no different than being unjust?

Crito: You speak truly.

Socrates: Neither, then, ought we return injustice nor do wrong to people, no matter what harm we may suffer from them. But see, Crito, that in accepting this principle, you do not agree to something that is contrary to your own opinion. For I know that few people think this principle is true or ever will think so. Those who accept it and those who do not share no common ground for discussion, but necessarily they look down upon one another because of the positions they hold. Consider very carefully whether you share this principle and opinion, and let us join in our reasoning from this starting point, that it is never right to act unjustly to another, nor to return a wrong, nor when suffering wrong to defend ourselves by doing wrong. Do you accept this or do you disagree and not share this principle? For I have long held this and I still do believe it, but if you have reached another conclusion, speak and teach it to me. But if you stay with the opinion we have stated, hear the next point.

Crito: But I do stay with it and share this principle, so speak.

Socrates: Then I will make the next point, or rather, I shall ask you: ought a person who has promised to do something that is just do it or break his promise?

Crito: He ought to do it.

Socrates: From what you have agreed, consider now what follows. If we leave this place and disobey the city, will we be wronging those whom we ought least to wrong, or not? And will we be staying with what we agreed was just, or not?

Crito: I cannot answer you, Socrates, for I don't understand.

Socrates: Then, consider it this way. What if as we were about to escape from here the Laws and Republic should stand before us and ask, "Tell me, Socrates, what do you have in mind to do by this act? Is it anything else than to destroy us the Laws and the whole state as far as you are able? Or do you think it is possible that a city can exist and not be overturned where the decisions of justice have no force, are made powerless, and are destroyed by private persons?" What shall we answer to these and other such questions, Crito? For there are many things someone could say, especially an orator, in defense of the law being broken, the law which declares that the decision of the court has authority. Or shall we answer them that the city has wronged us and did not judge the case correctly? Shall we say this or something else?

Crito: By Zeus, this is what we shall say, Socrates.

Socrates: What if the Laws say, "Socrates, is this the agreement you made with us, or is it to abide by the decisions which the city makes?"

The dialogue goes on to consider this issue, and Socrates shows how he had lived his life in such a way as to accept the benefits and authority of the city of Athens. Therefore, he concludes that if he escaped, he would be returning a wrong for a wrong, which, according to his principle, is unjust. This example from *Crito* is a good one, because it illustrates how important one's starting points are. Everything in the argument depends upon three principles: (1) that one ought not to do wrong, (2) nor do wrong in return for being wronged, (3) and, finally, that it is wrong to break an agreement. Seeing the force of these principles, Socrates asks Crito to consider very carefully whether he agrees to them or not before beginning his argument. In this way, Socrates is able to share the reasoning for his decision with his friend, taking him through the argument step by step.

The Method of Dialogue (Dialoguing Contrasted with Debating)

A debate is a way of presenting contrasting views on a particular question or issue. In political debates a question is usually asked, and the two candidates then are given an opportunity to respond. After their responses there is time given for a brief interchange between the two debaters. In a different style of debate, the debaters are given a larger block of time within which they can criticize each other and defend their own positions. Debates are a kind of competition that are also formally enacted by debating teams. In these situations, the rules are even more formalized. The primary difference between a debate and a dialogue is that debaters work *against* each other and dialogists work *with* each other.

In a dialogue it is important to establish what the question is and reach an agreement upon any important starting points, as we have discussed. One player may choose to state his position. In doing so, the person may follow the model of *Crito,* in which Socrates leads Crito through his reasoning by means of questioning. The more common approach is for the player to merely present a position, without questioning, while the other player listens. When the presenter has finished, it is important for the other party to make sure she understands what has been said. The best way is for the second person to attempt to summarize the position in her own words and let the first player consider whether or not she has understood. The presenter of the position must be the judge because he is the one trying to communicate the position. It is up to that person, therefore, to consider whether the communication was successful. If it was not successful, the dialogists must search out together where the logos was lost, discover why it was lost, and start again from that point. Once this is achieved, the second player can take on the role of questioner and explore and test the truth or falsity of the position.

In a debate, after one party has made his presentation, the second party is given her opportunity to make a rebuttal. This is the form of serious discussion with which we are most familiar. It is the basis of our legal system in the courts and also the means by which our legislators form laws—through competition. The competitive model, by its very nature, makes winning and losing of primary significance. Each party presents a view and his very self-image and reputation become tied to the position, so that as the debate progresses, it becomes a matter of pride to defend one's position as if it were one's possession. In this model the search for truth takes a backseat.

A dialogue takes a very different approach. After one party presents a viewpoint, the other party takes up the task of questioning and evaluating the position of the first. In order to do this, it is essential that the questioner put aside any beliefs on the issue so that she can function free of prejudice. This is, of course, an ideal goal and something we all can strive for. (There may be times, though, that one is unable to put one's views aside and feels compelled to say what one thinks. In these situations one ought to ask his partner to let him have the opportunity to briefly say what he thinks so that he can then return and explore the position presented.) Socrates is an ideal model because he says that he is in a state of emptiness and is therefore free to objectively consider any issue. This is not to say that he is a skeptic and has no vision of how to live; instead, this kind of emptiness is a profound state that liberates him from the attachment to beliefs (which is also the goal of Taoism and Buddhism).

At this point the questioner does not present another view. Instead, the goal is to draw out the implications of accepting the truth of the position. The job of the questioner is to draw out as clearly as possible the picture that would unfold if the position were accepted. One does this by asking questions that characterize the relationships inherent in the position. For example, if the topic is buying a house, how does buying a house relate to other closely related financial questions, like the purchase of a car or saving for children's education. The goal is to make as complete a picture as possible. Once this picture is drawn out, both parties can perceive much more clearly the nature of the situation and the truth or falsity or benefit or harm of accepting a certain position, path, or answer.

This way of proceeding is not competitive at all. The goal is not to show the other person to be wrong or right, but to help each other in the most friendly way to examine the issue as a whole. Ideally, if the procedure is done effectively, once the picture is drawn out for both parties to see, the truth or falsity of the position should become clearly evident. This is quite contrary to the spirit of a debate, in which one side poses as a knower or expert and seeks to convince the other about which position is right and which is wrong. The one doing the persuading functions on the assumption that he or she is the one who knows and that the other is ignorant. In dialogue, on the other hand, there is the ever-present recognition that any of us could possibly be wrong at any time, and so the best way to approach an issue is by working together toward the truth.

This approach in reasoning or logic has a formal name. It is called a *reductio ad absurdum* (literally, reduce to absurdity) argument. A *reductio* argument is one that seeks to prove its conclusion through indirect means. The reasoner assumes the truth of the opposite of a position and then goes on to show that a contradiction is implied or follows from this assumption; since a contradiction can't be true, the assumption or premise is proved false. Therefore, the reasoner may conclude that the opposite of the premise is true. For example, if one says, "It is raining," another may prove the first person wrong by saying, "Okay, let us assume that you are right and it is raining. Since it's raining, you must be getting wet." The other person agrees. "However, you are not getting wet. And that is a contradiction. Therefore, it must not be raining."

This is an example that illustrates the reasoning involved. Following is a more realistic example. Imagine a husband and wife arguing over whether to invite his family over for the weekend. The husband feels very strongly that his family should visit. The wife, however, is adamantly opposed. Let us say that the husband tells the wife that he is going to invite them because they have been promising to do so for the past month. Moreover, he says that the wife always invites her family and it is only right that he has his turn. Let us further imagine that the husband is getting worked up over the issue. At this point, if the wife were to present her views about the issue, the husband would clearly get very mad, and an argument would ensue. At this point, it would be much more effective to discuss the issue by employing the method of dialogue. The wife merely has to put her views aside and ask the husband to consider what will follow if the family comes to visit. Without even expressing a position, the husband will naturally consider what they will not be able to do. "We won't be able to do the needed repairs around the house, and we won't be able to play tennis." The couple then can consider together in an objective way which is the best plan for the weekend.

The point of the example is that when one can approach the discussion of an issue in this way, confrontation can be avoided. It is not always necessary to raise objections against a position. It is often much more effective to question others and explore the implications and difficulties that they themselves see in the position. This method establishes a friendly state in which the dialogue may take place, and in this state it is much easier to raise objections in a way that is not confrontational but helpful.

But simply using the *reductio* method does not make a discussion a dialogue. This kind of reasoning is also used in debates and courtrooms. The difference is that in a dialogue, one does not consciously employ this reasoning as a means to prove another wrong. That is not the goal of the questioner. The goal of the questioner is to draw out the implications of the position whether or not it turns out that what follows is contradictory or fits harmoniously with the original position. The questioner does not prejudge the issue. Even if she has a position, she does her best to put it aside. She takes no pleasure in proving the position true or false. She merely seeks to follow good reasoning. And so by proceeding in this way, the dialogists are not set in opposition, but instead are able to join together in the shared exploration.

Keeping It Together

An important practical issue that players in a dialogue must face is how to keep all the points and reasoning clear as the dialogue progresses. Few of us have developed the mental skills to do this. At one time, before tape recorders, computers, or even the ready access of ballpoint pens and paper, people trained their minds in listening skills and memory devices that enabled them to keep a dialogue in their minds very effectively. In the absence of this skill, it is essential that dialogists establish a way to keep track of their dialogue. One of the best ways to do this is to write out the key points and to draw diagrams that represent the relationships of the other points. This technique will help the dialogists stay focused on their goal, and it will also prevent miscommunication and misunderstanding, since both players can readily refer back to the key points that were made when disagreement arises. Both parties may choose to take notes, or one player may be assigned this role.

The Letter As an Invitation to Dialogue

Many of the dialogues that we partake in we enter because of a difficulty in a personal relationship with a friend, co-worker, family member, or lover. These kinds of dialogues often concern complicated issues that may even have a long history behind them. Such difficulties also very often bring out many emotions that make it more difficult for those involved to maintain the principles of a good dialogue. We will take up these important issues in chapters five, eight, and nine. One helpful suggestion can be made now. When you find yourself in one of these difficult situations, it can be helpful to invite the other person to engage in a dialogue in a letter. (This method can be used beneficially in any situation.)

In the letter you can take the same approach that we have been describing in this chapter. First of all, you can invite the other person to consider the issue with you in a friendly way in the spirit of dialogue, which means you recognize that either one of you may be wrong and together are seeking the truth of the issue. Second, you need to introduce the question or issue as you understand it. Third, you can present your view of the issue and ask the other person to consider it. Finally, you can request that the two of you find an appropriate time to sit down and pursue the truth of the issue together as a dialogue, taking turns in the roles of questioner and answerer, hearing each other out and exploring the issue as friends.

4 THE IDEAL OF TRUTH

Truth

The ultimate goal of a dialogue is to discover the truth. All human beings are rightfully lovers of truth, though many of us become misdirected. Dialogue is a way of declaring one's concern for this noble ideal and sharing it with others. It is a means of restoring integrity to our individual lives, relationships, and society. In this chapter we explore the classical Greek vision of philosophy as the love of truth, then contrast this vision with the skepticism, relativism, and pragmatism that pervade contemporary thinking, presenting an imposing block to philosophical idealism. Finally, we consider Plato's *divided line*, a structure that we can use to identify different kinds of claims to knowledge, which is essential to the integrity of dialogue.

When we declare our concern for truth, it necessarily becomes a higher principle in our lives—a principle that is genuinely sacred. Many seek for the return of the sacred in their lives by looking in the most distant places, cultures, languages, and traditions. Honoring Truth is a much simpler way to begin and much closer to home, though, perhaps a greater challenge. When one honors Truth, genuine sacrifice is demanded—the sacrifice of what is false.

The whole ritual of animal sacrifice, as it is expressed in the Greek mythic tradition, is a symbol for the sacrifice of what is false. The tradition of sacrifice was given to man by the Prometheus. Prometheus (whose name means "forethought") is the demigod who stole fire from the altar of Zeus to give to man. Prometheus taught man to wrap the bones and vittles in fat and to burn them upon the altar as an offering to the gods. By wrapping the unwanted parts of the slain animal in this way, he showed humankind how they could give offerings to the gods while preserving what they needed for their subsistence. In its literal form, the myth presents Prometheus teaching human beings to fool the gods, but the myth represents the idea that the gods accept as an offering what *appears* to be real and allow human beings to keep what is *truly* real.

The fire that Prometheus brought to humankind represents the power of the mind, and so Prometheus is said to have also given us the rational arts. A rational art is any art that uses knowledge to predict and plan for a future benefit. In the respect that such arts look to the future, they are the work of foresight. In the healing arts, one of which we call medicine, a doctor examines a patient and then establishes a therapy that will help the patient return to a state of health. In this art, the healer must be able to distinguish the true from the false so that he or she can discern what merely appears to be healthy but is not. Moreover, in order for the patient to gain the benefit of the rational art, he or she must be willing to give up the false to the sacrificial flames. For example, in our world there are foods that appear good with respect to their taste and the pleasure they produce and foods that are truly good in contributing to the health of the body. Those who have a heart condition and are facing the clogging of their arteries and imminent heart attack must be willing to sacrifice these unhealthy foods for those foods that are truly good. By such a sacrifice the person is able to live a life more in accordance with the ideal of health, and in this way honors the gods (in Greek terms) and the truth by living a more ideal life.

In order to honor the truth, it is often the case that we must be willing to give up something we desire, and these objects of desire wield power over us. We are all attracted to worldly goods in some way—whether it be money, power, success, or sex. Each of these possesses an image of benefit and of goodness that attracts us. In his life, Socrates used the art of dialogue as a means to question what the nature of the true good is; the goal of his questioning was to achieve a clearer vision of the true good so that humans could better perceive the truth in the personal choices they make, for our decisions in life center upon this very issue—what is it that we suppose to be good? In Socrates' analysis, the nature of all human error lies in supposing what is *not* good to *be* good. In other words, what leads humans to harm themselves and others are false beliefs about what is good. For example, the alcoholic is possessed by a belief that the pleasure of drunkenness is a greater good than sobriety, and the tyrant is possessed by the belief that the pleasure of power and ruling others is a greater good than a life of justice. In many cases, the nature of the specific beliefs that are functioning are more subtle and complex, fitting in a very sophisticated way into one's upbringing in the family, but the principle is the same; at the root of so-called evil in our world is human ignorance. We say "so-called evil" because, according to Plato and Socrates, the very condition for a bad or harmful action is a desire for the good.

The goal of life, according to Socrates, is to gain a vision of goodness so that one can free oneself from the kind of ignorance that leads to harm. In order to gain such a vision of goodness, one must consider seriously the nature of humankind. For Socrates, the true life of humans is the life of the soul, and Plato's *Republic* lays out Socrates' picture of the soul and what constitutes its true excellence and good. Socrates is challenged by his friend Glaucon to demonstrate that the life of the just man, the one who honors Truth, is better than the life of the unjust man, and Glaucon sets up this challenge in the following way. He seeks to discover what justice and injustice are, the power that each has, and their power in the soul of the human being. He further requires that Socrates show that the just life is better, independent of any worldly benefits one may receive from being just. If the just life is truly better than the unjust life, Glaucon demands that it be demonstrated to be better under all circumstances—even when the just man has none of the worldly benefits of justice, but suffers all the troubles of one with a reputation for injustice, hatred, imprisonment, torture, and so on, whereas, the unjust man receives all the worldly benefits of his injustice—money, power, sex—and gains a reputation for the greatest justice. This constitutes a remarkable challenge, and one that Socrates takes on in heroic fashion. His demonstration comprises the second through tenth books of Plato's philosophical masterpiece. I am not going to attempt to summarize Socrates' answer. Instead, readers are encouraged to delve into this study for themselves. In the most simple way, though, Socrates says that one chooses justice over injustice because of one's concern for higher principles and ideals.

On the other hand, people choose the life of injustice and deceit for the most part to get something they want but believe they can't obtain, or something that is more difficult to get by being honest, whether it be money, success, power, or sex. Thus, to honor the truth means simply to be willing to sacrifice these things for the higher ideals of life. A just man, therefore, holds that one's inner life, the world of the psyche, is where one's true well-being resides and that one cannot gain the true good by becoming immersed in falsehood in any way. An ancient philosophical maxim says, "As we live through the soul, it must be said that by virtue of this we live well; just as, since we see through the eyes, it is by virtue of these that we see well." The just man is able to gain a degree of transcendence or freedom from the pleasures and pains of the material world by recognizing that the higher good of these ideals presents a more real, genuine, and lasting good than those of the lower desires; with this transcendence he is afforded a degree of freedom from material concerns and gains the power to live a more ideal life. Plato and Socrates, however, were not ascetics. They did not reject the concerns and pleasures of the material world, but instead they recognized the difference between higher and lower goods and ordered their lives accordingly.

In the *Republic,* Plato characterizes the philosopher as one who possesses many qualities; the most important of them is the love of truth. Plato says that the philosopher is a hater of falsehood whether it be in large or small matters. The philosopher disdains falsehood, because falsehood is what covers up and hides what is real. Now it is reasonable for those who are not familiar with philosophy to ask why such an individual would have this kind of love and devotion for the true and the real. For most people, reality is considered to be something rather awful. Although our lives are filled with love and beauty, such things as pain, disease, conflict, and death seem to have the upper hand. The philosopher, however, cultivates the mind to recognize the greater source of goodness and excellence that orders the drama of human life. He aims to gain a direct vision of this divine power, which in Plato's cosmology is the cause of all existence. Thus, the goal of philosophy is to realize directly that every aspect of human life and existence is both excellent and good.

Although philosophers and mystics declare that the achievement of this goal lies within the grasp of each of us, few take this path, and fewer still accomplish it. Nonetheless, one does not have to be an accomplished mystic to recognize the remarkable power of the True and the Real in human life. It can be easily appreciated if we consider the issue with regard to the human character. Consider a beautiful man or woman, the kind who appears to walk off the cover of a fashion magazine. Such a person certainly appears to be beautiful, and that kind of beauty has a remarkable power to draw out attention, desire, and possibly love. Yet this is physical beauty. Consider how much more powerful another kind of beauty is, the beauty of the soul.

The beauty of the soul far outweighs physical beauty. For if we were to discover that this physically beautiful person was a really awful human being—one who consistently lied and hurt other people, for example—whatever power his or her physical beauty had over us would quickly vanish. (There are times, though, when one is unwilling to give up that appearance and so refuses to fully acknowledge what one sees about his or her beloved's soul in order to preserve the other as a beloved.) And yet, if there is someone with just a modicum of physical beauty, but who is a sincere, joyous person filled with the love of life, it is likely that we would be very drawn to that person either as a lover or friend. The power of beauty and the excellence of the human soul are seen also in the kinds of people we most admire.

People of genuine excellence and greatness truly inspire awe, and these are the kinds of people who are immortalized both in history and the world of fiction as the great human heroes.

In each of our own lives in every decision we make, we have the opportunity to act with the genuineness and integrity of a true hero. We continually face the same challenge that Glaucon presents to Socrates, that is, whether to live a just life or an unjust life. We face this challenge in small ways and in large ways, and both are equally significant because each decision we make shapes the nature of who we are. It may be a simple matter of not speaking up when a cashier charges us a lower price than is marked for an item in a store or the bigger issue of lying in order to keep a job or get a promotion. In these situations there is an opportunity to gain worldly good, but to take it we must take on a false appearance. In the moment that we accept a false appearance, we abandon the path of excellence and deteriorate in some way.

There are also the more challenging scenes where we are faced with a situation in which we don't like what's going on and desire to speak our minds about the truth of the matter. However, to do so presents great risks. Perhaps we want to address an issue with a husband or wife, mother or father, or friend, but we realize that doing so will be very difficult for the other person and may jeopardize the entire relationship. Or it could be a situation at work where we know the act of speaking out may cost us our job and livelihood. These are situations that demand much courage. But both of these cases are placed in their proper perspective when we compare them with the kinds of situations in which honoring the truth and speaking freely may threaten one's very life or the life of a loved one. This is the case for those who confront tyranny and injustice in criminal or tyrannical political situations. In these confrontations, the greatest risk is at stake and, consequently, the greatest challenge to one's ideals and principles.

In contemporary technocratic society, few of us encounter such imposing dangers in our lives. Instead, we are faced with much smaller challenges, and although these challenges are smaller for our particular lives, they are of much greater significance for humanity as a whole. In our world today, dishonesty is often expected. Students cheat in school, taxpayers regularly lie about their taxes, lawyers typically lie about the law, politicians often lie about politics, journalists sometimes lie about events; employers commonly lie to employees, employees lie to employers, salesman lie to customers, husbands and wives lie to each other, parents lie to their children, children lie to their parents, and clergy even lie to their congregations. There is nothing out of the ordinary about the lies that we tell and the false appearances that most of us put on. In fact, it may be more out of the ordinary to discover someone who actually tells the truth. The state of society is so bad that even many who do not want to live such a life have begun to believe that there is no other way of surviving in the world today. Many have adopted the Macheavelian formula that "the ends justify the means." Yet this is a rationalization for one's injustice and dishonesty, claiming that it is all right to abandon truth on the way to some good end. But one must consider that even if this good end is achieved, the unjust and dishonest means one uses bring further injustice and dishonesty into our world. Individuals who choose this path must accept this falsehood in their lives and the state of mind and lack of excellence that it fosters, thus contributing to the greater power of falsehood in our world as a whole.

It is especially difficult today for individuals to follow their ideals and principles because we live in a society that has accepted this "ends justifies the means" formula. We have abandoned the notion that there is a higher ideal that can unite human beings in their communities in their efforts toward a common good and instead have reduced social relations to the lowest common denominator—competition and greed. Competition and greed are not good in themselves, but they are used by our society for what we perceive to be a good end—the accumulation of wealth, consumerism, and the further industrialization of our planet. We have settled for this kind of society because we have inherited a skeptical tradition of political philosophy that denies that social communities can aspire to higher ideals. Skepticism in many forms pervades our world.

Skepticism and two closely related doctrines called relativism and pragmatism are modes of belief that oppose philosophical dialogue. Skepticism is the view that the truth cannot be discovered or that it does not even exist. Skepticism is closely related to relativism, which holds that there is no absolute truth and goes on to say that whatever anyone *thinks* is true *is* true. However, this kind of truth is not truth at all, but merely individual belief. Thus, the relativist denies the existence of an objective truth and says that the only thing that exists is personal belief, then goes on to rename personal belief as truth. The pragmatist does something similar. He also says that genuine truth does not exist, but that what works or is effective in a situation can be called truth. Pragmatism is a school of philosophy that emerged in the United States and has an academic and scientific form. But it is also a worldly view with which most are familiar. It is the view that one does not worry about ideals but instead focuses on the worldly and the practical. Each of these views presents distinct blocks to genuine dialogue and the philosophical life, blocks that we must consider.

Relativism

Relativism either halts dialogue in midstream or precludes it by declaring that the only meaningful activity for those who disagree is to compare and appreciate their differing views; accordingly, relativism declares that it is impolite or "politically incorrect" to challenge or question another's beliefs. There are various reasons why people hold such a view. One is that they believe that challenging and questioning threaten the rights of others to maintain their beliefs. Another is that they fear that if the door is open to this kind of discussion, it will escalate into hostility and confrontation. A third, and perhaps the most important reason is that relativists reject the idea that there is a standard or measure that we can use to judge beliefs, and so one person's or group's belief is as good as another. Moreover, they often hold that different individuals and groups gain their beliefs from their particular backgrounds and cultures, so that each has an equal right to exist and is valid by virtue of its historical existence. A corollary to this view is that no one can truly understand the belief of another, since we each have different backgrounds and/or different cultural and religious upbringings. Ultimately, we think that each of our beliefs is a perspective that emerges from our unique personal and cultural experiences, expressed in the adages "Whatever seems true to anyone is true to him to whom it seems so," "To each his own," and "Perception is knowledge." It is a position that has had a resurgence as part of the movement in favor of political correctness, but it has a history that goes back thousands of years. Its most famous exponent was the Sophist of ancient Greece called Protagoras, who said, "Man is the measure of all things."

Relativism challenges the first principle of the model of dialogue. The relativists declare that objective truth does not exist. A variation would be the skeptic's view that we can't know the truth, so we shouldn't judge or question others' beliefs. Our culture is pervaded by relativism, and we all accept the relativist position to some degree. However, philosophers have traditionally presented a number of arguments against the legitimacy of this position, and, in his play *Is It All Relative?*, Pierre Grimes has demonstrated that, in essence, the relativist's position is a prejudice.

Knowledge As Perception

From this viewpoint, relativism takes this form: "If it is perceived to be true, then it is true." The relativist here holds that since each person's perception is unique, it follows that no one can judge another's perception as false. If we try to apply this position, a number of unacceptable conclusions result. For example, if someone perceives the earth to be flat, does that mean that the earth is flat simply because the person perceives it to be so? And does it also follow that the sun revolves around the earth because it appears that way to perceivers? Clearly these conclusions don't follow. Another example is the phenomenon of the refraction of water. Straight objects appear to be bent when perceived through the medium of water. Does that mean that they are bent within the water and not bent when they come out of the water? Of course not. In the world of physical perception, there are standards that we use to judge the truth and falsity of our perceptions. We distinguish between those who are nearsighted and those who have good eyesight and also between those who are color-blind and those who perceive colors correctly. There are objective standards by which we measure the accuracy of perception.

Standards

The relativist may also apply his or her position to areas in which it is claimed that there are no measures or standards by which one can judge. Relativism is a widely held belief in the realm of music and art. Although it is rare for people to say that perceptions are relative in the face of the counterexamples presented earlier, it is more typical for them to hold the relativist position that beauty is in the eye of the beholder; in the case of music, perhaps we ought to say, "Beautiful music is in the ear of the listener."

If someone thinks that there are no true standards for good music, for example, and that it is merely a matter of personal taste, there are also a number of difficulties that follow. If a person thinks the screeching of chalk on a blackboard is as beautiful as Mozart, does this perception make it so? Is there a difference between musical sound and plain noise? Consider the different power of each. What effect does each have on the listener? It has been demonstrated that students who listen to Mozart before taking mathematics tests do better than those who do not. This is because Mozart composed his music according to musical figures that are analogous to beautiful mathematical patterns. At the same time, the music does not follow a mere formula but utilizes these patterns in a highly creative and unique way. One who listens to classical music is able to study the nature of the form and gain a greater appreciation. The appreciation of classical music can be nurtured through the development of the mind. On the other hand, there are other types of music that are presented in simplistic forms, and if one studies them and becomes more familiar with them, they gain a greater monotony. These forms do not enhance the mind, but instead dull it.

Some may claim to enjoy the monotony or the disturbing sounds of certain kinds of music, but though they may appear to take joy in it, does that fact make the object truly enjoyable? There are people who take pleasure in pain, but we do not then conclude that those painful experiences are pleasurable simply because the masochist perceives them to be so. Instead, we recognize that masochists have an illness that blocks them from experiencing the world in a natural way. Similarly, people claim that there are forms of "musical" expression that use sounds that are disturbing to the mind of the listener and they say that it is music, or perhaps even beautiful. But the very nature of beauty is to draw and attract the human being, not to disturb and repulse one. This power of beauty to draw us in and elevate the mind is a standard that can be used to judge music.

Standards, in any form of art, provide a measure of the richness and depth of an art form and indicate the degree to which a work and its beauty can be studied, appreciated, and grasped more profoundly. One might ask, if there are clear standards for what is beautiful in music and art, why doesn't everyone agree about what is most beautiful? In reality, those most learned in art and music do agree about who the true geniuses and masters of these fields are in history, figures like Leonardo da Vinci and Johann Sebastian Bach. However, in any particular field there can be agreement only to the degree that the masters of those fields recognize the specificity of the standards used to judge the work. In classical times, the Greeks were very concerned about articulating these criteria very specifically so that works could be judged, and there was agreement about the true masters in each field: Homer in epic poetry, Aeschylus in tragedy, Aristophanes in comedy, Plato in philosophy, Phidias in sculpture. The specificity of criteria allowed this culture to produce the greatest artistic geniuses, geniuses who are recognized to be unrivaled in history. It was for this very reason that the great artists of fifteenth-century Italy sought to recapture the classical spirit, because they recognized the power of this approach to art and life.

When an individual or society declares standards, the standards become a measure for one's growth. Without a standard, there is no way to judge. With a standard, one can recognize how far one has come and where one's limitations are—and then strive to go beyond them. With standards, one can recognize where one gets stuck and can thus explore the nature of the difficulty and the block to one's growth. Without standards, one does not take on this challenge. The conscious articulation of standards for a culture or for oneself can therefore be a powerful means toward growth and development. One ought not fear that one's standards are imperfect and so be hindered from establishing them. It is only by putting one's standards and ideals into words that one can bring them to birth, see them, and have the opportunity to evaluate them. As we grow, it is likely that our understanding of our own ideals and standards will grow as well.

Historical and Cultural Determinism

The belief that everything is bound by its specific historical and cultural conditions is a restricting one. It is evident that we are in many respects shaped by these conditions; however, it is very different to state that we are restricted and limited to them. This is what is implied by those who claim that one cannot truly understand another cultural perspective. It means that we cannot transcend our own perspective to see another's clearly. But if we do not have the capacity to transcend our cultural, historical, and religious upbringing, our growth and development as human beings are circumscribed by the limitations of that upbringing. But this is to establish arbitrary boundaries on growth and understanding. It is a way of defining the human being as a historically bound creature. It literally prejudges the extent of our growth. It is a dangerous belief because it has the power to convince others that they cannot transcend the limitations that their backgrounds have placed on them. And yet people of all different backgrounds and times have been able to achieve the whole range of human accomplishments. Although it may be very difficult to go beyond these borders or limitations, it is possible.

The interesting thing about the ancient Greek culture, which is not commonly known today, is that it was not restricted to those of Greek heritage. The Greeks recognized that the basis of their culture was a universal ideal for humanity, based on the cultivation of excellence and learning. As Aristotle said, "to be Hellenic is a state of mind." Thus, the Hellenic cultural ideal was one that was freely chosen by many Jewish, Egyptian, Indian, Arabic, and Roman peoples in the ancient world, who incorporated it into the life of their communities.

Rhetoric

Oftentimes the relativist position is used rhetorically. Since it has the force of a common belief, many people often appeal to it to end a discussion they don't like by using one of these familiar phrases: "It's all subjective anyway" or "You have your opinion, and I have mine." In these situations, a dialogist can explain to the other speaker the nature of dialogue as a search for objective standards that can be agreed upon by each person and that can be used to evaluate beliefs and opinions. The person asserting the relativist position can choose to enter into such a dialogue or not. If he is not interested in such a dialogue, he may be interested in a dialogue about the position that things are all relative. If so, this can be the topic for a very interesting exploration. In such a dialogue, the questioner may choose to investigate the reasons why the other person holds the position. What are its merits, and how did the person derive the position? Does he or she apply it to all topics or just to certain ones? If just to certain ones, on what basis does he or she make that distinction? For a further exploration of such a dialogue, the reader will certainly enjoy Plato's *Theaetetus* or Pierre Grimes's contemporary play *Is It All Relative?* based on the *Theaetetus*.

Prejudice

In *Is It All Relative?*, the position that "whatever seems to be true to a person *is* true because to him it seems so" is explored in a formal fashion by the characters of the play. Through their exploration, they discover that if the person holding this position is asked on what basis she makes her judgment that her view is true, she can answer only, "Because it seems so." However, the phrase *seems so* is an essential part of the position; whatever seems true is true because it *seems so*. Therefore, the relativist cannot give an explanation for her position that is different from her very position, and this violates one of the most important principles of reasoning—the principle that states that a viewpoint must be based on or supported by a statement of evidence that is different from the position being held. When this rule is violated, it is termed "circular reasoning." In circular reasoning, one defends one's position by restating the position. For example, if someone claims that the New York Mets are going to win the World Series and you ask the person to explain this prediction, it would be circular reasoning if he or she said, "Because the Mets are the best baseball team in the major leagues." A good explanation must state why the Mets are the best team.

In a further analysis, the characters in the play consider what would happen if someone held that the relativist position is false. In such a case the relativist would not accept that what seems true to the other person is true (namely, that the position is false). Thus, he would deny the truth of the other's judgment and thereby contradict his very position that *"whatever* seems true to anyone is true to him to whom it seems so." In this way it is made clear that the one who holds the relativist position can accept only the judgments of those who agree with his position and not the judgments of those who disagree with him. Therefore, the characters in Grimes's play who are evaluating the position conclude that the relativist position is a prejudice. They define a prejudice as something that is asserted as true but cannot be either proved or disproved, believed in and insisted upon even after its inadequacies become visible, and yet cannot be rejected.* This is a general definition of prejudice that covers the whole class of prejudices (racial, religious, and so on). The prejudice we are considering here is a prejudice against the use

---

*Pierre Grimes, *Is It All Relative?* (Costa Mesa, California: Hyparxis Press, 1995), p. 32.

of the mind and critical thinking, since the relativist position denies the legitimacy of evaluation, judgment, and the search for genuine truth and knowledge. Instead, it declares that all is belief.

The position of relativism satisfies the criteria of the definition of prejudice. (1) It is asserted as a universal truth by those who proclaim it. (2) It is not something that can be proved or disproved, because the relativist declares that what seems true to her in her personal experience *is* true and that such a thing is not open to proof or disproof because it is experienced only by a particular person. (3) Relativism, in its various forms, raises a host of contradictions. (4) Those who hold this view are often unwilling to let go of the belief even when the contradictions are made clear.

Consequences of Relativism

There are a number of very harmful consequences for both the individual and the society that accepts the relativist position. For one, if a society like the United States accepts the view that cultures are ultimately separated from one another by their perspectives, it leads to the inevitable isolation of communities and hinders the ability of peoples to interrelate—a problem which is becoming more and more evident. Moreover, it raises the prejudgement that there is necessarily going to be conflict between both races and religions, since each society thinks differently. It rejects the idea that common principles and ideals exist that can unite people and that are universal and more significant than one's particular cultural identity. To accept a universal ideal does not mean that one need give up or abandon his cultural background. It means that one seeks a shared ideal that is common to all humans. For despite the diversity of religions and cultures, most share a general agreement about what it means to live a virtuous and excellent life and how to treat other human beings. This does not mean that one has to give up the diversity of habits and customs and preferences that make each culture unique and interesting. It means that cultures can together seek a higher ideal.

At the same time, there exists a very real danger of conflict between different religions and their cultures because all cultures possess some degree of prejudice and falsity that needs to be recognized and from which individuals and communities need to free themselves. Many thinkers, most notably Samuel P. Huntington in the article "The Clash of Civilizations," have expressed the belief that particular cultural and religious differences are the greatest source of political conflict in the present and the future. Thus, the pursuit of common ideals is an essential way to seek to bring greater understanding to humanity, especially because the future well-being of all of us has become so interdependent. Therefore, a global dialogue is becoming a vital key to our future.

Skepticism

Relativism is closely connected to skepticism. People believe that all is relative because they do not think that there is any universal knowledge within our grasp. For some, it is because they do not think such knowledge exists. Others are willing to consider the possibility that it exists, but nevertheless believe that such knowledge can never be reached by humankind. Skepticism is accompanied by a certain state of mind that many believe to be the primary mark of intellectual integrity. Most individuals in academia are confirmed skeptics to one degree or another. In fact, to think that one can grasp an eternal and absolute truth is often looked upon by academics as a mark of naïveté. Consequently, many academics find it to be their very purpose to protect the contemporary culture of skepticism. They feel that skepticism is a healthy principle because it generates a tolerance for the multiplicity of possible views and approaches to issues and protects society against the threat of dogmatism and absolutism. Although it is important to maintain a tolerance that allows the free exploration of ideas and to protect against authoritarianism, the irony is that the skeptics have become the authorities and skepticism their protected dogma.

What academics most reject is what is called speculative thinking. Speculative thinking appeals to principles to explain something without physical evidence of its truth. In a dialogue about a meaningful topic, one must often appeal to principles that are based upon speculation. For example, if we were talking about the meaning of life, we might lay down the principle that if life is meaningful, it must be good and must be directly relevant to each of us as individuals. And while this a likely principle, and it may be the basis of agreement for a very interesting dialogue, such a principle is considered unprovable and therefore unwarranted in an academic discussion. Consequently, much that is important or essential to human life is excluded accordingly. In fact, all ancient Wisdom traditions are based on this kind of speculative thinking (in conjunction with spiritual experience) and therefore are excluded from academic and scientific discussions of truth.

In pursuing such a profound topic as the meaning of life—or even a question of more personal or practical significance, as "What career ought I pursue?"—we may often feel skeptical and believe that the answer is beyond our grasp. We may encounter a voice that doubts that we can ever come to know such a thing. Such skeptical voices from others or from within our own heads can debilitate us. They can cut off an exploration or our enthusiasm for pursuing a question, issue, or goal before it even begins. In a famous encounter with a young Greek Sophist named Meno, Socrates is confronted with the skeptical challenge. Socrates has a very pertinent reply to Meno, one we can use as a model for the skeptical voices that we encounter in our own life. He says to Meno: "We are better, braver and less idle in thinking that there's a need to search for what we don't know than we are if we think that it's not even possible to discover what we don't know, nor even necessary to search. Now for this, I would fight with all my strength as far as I am able in both word and deed." His contention against the skeptic is a simple one. If we think we cannot know, then we will not seek for what we desire to know, and we will instead be idle and therefore will certainly never come to know. However, the belief that we can't know is a prejudice. It prejudges that we cannot know before we even try.

The same point is vital to our dialogues today. Dialogists ought to approach their search eager to discover what they long to know, and in this way they will be more likely to put in the energy needed for the quest. If they come to the search skeptical that they cannot work together or that what they are seeking to discover cannot be found, these kinds of thoughts will only hinder the exploration. It is important to keep in mind that any sincere exploration done with integrity yields some benefit to the dialogists (further clarity of the question, insight, or recognition of false beliefs) whether or not what they ultimately seek is discovered.

Structure of Knowledge

Western civilization since the time of the scientific revolution has been centered upon the pursuit and development of knowledge. In many ways, the pursuit of knowledge has replaced religion as the unifying cultural principle of the West. Traditionally, knowledge has been sought as something that is certain and indubitable, as Descartes says. In many ways the indubitable character of knowledge has been at the center of the West's cultural myth of science. In the twentieth century, though, this myth has been shattered.

Mathematics and science provide us with the two most familiar models of knowing. We discussed earlier Euclid's model. In this model, claims of mathematical knowledge are the result of reasoning that is based upon accepted definitions and axioms. Our most basic geometrical knowledge comes from Euclid's work—for example, the fact that all the angles of a triangle are equal to the sum of two right angles or, as we say today, 180 degrees. As we explained earlier, this conclusion is only as strong as the foundation it rests upon, and this foundation in the definitions and axioms is never proved.

The same conclusion follows in empirical science. All scientific knowledge derives from the mathematical analysis of data from experimentation. Every scientific claim is built upon the definitions and axioms of mathematical systems as well as the definitions and axioms of the scientific system used to evaluate the data. Each scientific claim of knowledge is recognized by scientists to be, in reality, the best current theory or explanation of the data. In principle, every theory is capable of being surpassed. No scientific claim is ever conclusive, because there is always the possibility of finding a better theory to explain the data or the chance that new data could emerge that the original theory cannot explain.

From a philosophical point of view, there is a further challenge to science. Science makes claims about physical phenomena, but the philosopher asks, "Do scientists really know what matter is?" Not at all. In their view, matter is energy and energy matter, and they don't truly know what either is. They merely study the patterns of effects of energy/matter in nature, but they don't know what it is in itself. Despite these criticisms, we generally call the claims of mathematicians and scientists "knowledge." This is because scientists proceed according to accepted methods of observation and analyze their observations according to mathematical systems. In this respect, they work toward their conclusions in a reasonable manner and seek out the confirmation of their peers. Clearly these rational procedures give science a significance that other kinds of claims do not always have. At the same time, however, science faces very real limitations, most especially in any claim to certainty.

There is also a commonsense form of knowledge. We say that we "know" things when we ourselves experience them directly. There are a host of famous skeptical arguments about this kind of knowledge as well. Sense experience is clearly fallible. However, despite such doubts, the truth is that we will always function in the physical world according to what we experience through our senses. This is the basis of our survival. The key is that it is through our senses. Since we are able to perceive with five different senses, we can evaluate our experience with our minds. We do not rely wholly on what our senses report to us because we recognize that our senses are not completely trustworthy, though with the use of reason they help us satisfy our material needs in the world.

We grant the use of the term "knowledge" to mathematics, science, and common sense because of the reliability we find in these sources. Commonsense knowledge is wholly based on sense experience. Mathematics, on the other hand, is based on logic and our ideas of the different kinds of mathematical objects, like number and figure, and not on sense experience at all (except, perhaps, for some modern mathematics). Empirical science is a kind of mix of these two. It uses the formal systems of math and logic to evaluate sense experience. Each of these three sources, however, is not a source for absolute truth or certainty in any way. Whereas science and math must rely on the assumptions of a system, science and common sense are dependent upon the fallible nature of sense perception.

In dialogue, it is essential to have an appreciation for the basis of the knowledge claims that people make, whether they arise from personal experience, science, mathematics, or logic. In our society, we have the tendency to accept knowledge claims as unquestionable (especially when they come from so-called experts), when, in truth, each is based on an assumption and is liable to error to a greater or lesser degree. In a dialogue, one must be sure to recognize when one accepts certain claims as true, for then these claims become axioms upon which the dialogue rests. By recognizing that these purported claims to knowledge have a degree of fallibility, we do not rest certain with our conclusions; we leave open the possibility for further dialogue and the exploration of other, rival "knowledge" claims. By accepting the statements of scientific experts as certain, we close off the very real possibility that the experts could be wrong, and we may put too much trust in a conclusion that does not rest on the surest grounds. We may blindly assume that the scientists cannot be wrong and later end up disappointed. All the same, it is necessary and reasonable to give a certain degree of trust to these kinds of knowledge claims; otherwise, we would have difficulty functioning in our technological society. The point here is not to criticize these kinds of claims to knowledge, but instead to recognize them for what they are and not to expect more than they can offer.

Pragmatism

Pragmatism is the twentieth century's response to the critique of knowledge. The pragmatist accepts the criticisms and flaws of science and defends the commonsense and scientific claims to knowledge by saying, "Since these sources help us function in the world and are generally accepted, it is appropriate to call them truth and knowledge." The pragmatist abandons the traditional standards for truth and knowledge and accepts the imperfect claims that worldly experience makes. In this regard, the pragmatist is also a skeptic. He does not seek out another form of knowledge that does satisfy the standards for genuine knowledge. He is not a philosopher in the traditional sense because he abandons ideals and the pursuit of truth in the acceptance of an impostor.

Plato's Divided Line

In Plato's philosophy, the types of knowledge we have been discussing are not called knowledge at all, for the reasons presented. Instead, mathematics, for example, is called understanding, since understanding is not something that claims to be absolutely certain but is something that can admit of varying degrees. Whereas knowledge claims to be absolute, certain, and final, understanding is an ongoing process in which we seek to gain greater clarity and recognize our limitations. At the same time, it requires that one appeal to reasonable methods and standards in one's exploration, evaluations, and conclusions.

Plato reserves the term *knowledge* for something that is complete and perfect, and that is the direct realization of the nature of reality in what today we call a mystical experience. On the path toward that kind of knowledge, Plato distinguishes four different types of functioning of the mind and four corresponding objects. We can represent Plato's idea in a simple analogy that Grimes has adopted from Plato's *Meno* and *Republic*. Imagine you want to take a trip from Los Angeles to San Francisco. On the lowest level of the use of the mind, what Plato calls *image thinking*, you would not be able to discern the difference between an imagined road and a real one.

The next level of the use of the mind is called *opinion*. If you have never been to San Francisco and have not seen a map of it, you would have no basis for making a judgment about which road is the correct one to take to San Francisco. You could have an opinion about which road to take, and that opinion could be true or false, but the opinion would not have any rational basis.

Understanding is the next level and is distinguished by the possession of reasoning. To continue the example, then, if you looked at a map and based your judgment upon reading it—and you read it correctly—you could be said to possess a true opinion. Since this true opinion is founded on a rational basis, it is called *understanding*.

The highest level of the functioning of the mind Plato calls *knowledge*. If you went on to follow the map to San Francisco, with this experience of seeing the road for yourself, you could be said to be in a state of knowing how to go to San Francisco.

Thus, Plato distinguishes four states of the mind with respect to one's level of functioning:

> Knowledge
> Understanding
> Opinion
> Image Thinking

At the first level one cannot distinguish an image or fantasy from the physical world, so that the corresponding object of the mind is images. In the second case, one does distinguish image from physical object, but one does not use intellect to judge according to rational standards. At this level, the object of the mind is one's opinions about the physical world, opinions independent of a rational basis. On the level of understanding, one still functions with opinions, but one bases one's opinions upon a standard and therefore is able to use the mind to examine this kind of rational object. Finally, at the level of knowledge, one experiences directly for oneself the truth toward which the reasoning points.

In our example, one not only follows the map but also discovers the true object that the map describes. On a spiritual path, there can also be a rational map, which is what a Wisdom tradition aims to present. Many traditions give guides to the stages of spiritual development. In Zen, there is the famous maxim that says, "Don't confuse the finger pointing to the moon with the moon itself." This idea is also expressed in the Zen saying "The map is not the territory."

The point is that the guide is not the thing itself. Accordingly, many spiritual traditions hold the view that the rational description of the nature of reality is no longer an important goal for one who has the experience. In the Platonic tradition, the cultivation of the understanding of both the map and the territory is the primary means of the philosopher's further spiritual development and the deepening of his or her enlightenment. (Plato goes on to give a more detailed discussion of the structure of knowledge in the section on the divided line at the end of the sixth book of the *Republic* and then to illustrate these ideas presents his famous allegory of the cave at the beginning of the seventh book.)

The existence of the accomplished philosophers and mystics is the greatest standard and measure of our own lives and the greatest challenge to the relativists, skeptics, and pragmatists. Whereas the skeptics claim that such spiritual experiences are beyond the grasp of humans, the experience of the world's mystics presents the boldest refutation of this claim. Whereas the relativists believe that truth is subjective, the most interesting thing about the comparative study of mysticism is the remarkable similarity and commonality of the descriptions of the leading mystics in all the world's religious and philosophical traditions (a view that even the materialist philosopher Bertrand Russell attests to). The universality of mystical experience is strong evidence in support of its truth. It also tells us that none of us should submit to the skeptic's belief that spiritual matters are impossible to know, but instead that we should eagerly search, as Socrates commands. Finally, it reveals that what is worldly or practical, according to the pragmatist, is not. Instead, it shows that what is truly important are the deeper longings for truth and a more ideal life.

5 THE HUMAN DRAMA

The Human Drama

When we engage in a dialogue, we enter into a relationship with another human being, and this relationship is the most important aspect of any dialogue. Whatever issues, beliefs, or questions emerge in our dialogues, their significance always rests on the way these ideas relate to human life. This personal element and its accompanying drama are the most meaningful and challenging part of dialogue.

There is a necessary drama that accompanies dialogue because our encounters with people and ideas affect us. They have a power to put us in different states of mind—concern, worry, joy, puzzlement, and anger. When one enters a state of joy, for example, one does not remain in that state. Joy, like all other states, subsides, and there is the inevitable transition to other states of mind. The movement from one state to another forms the dynamic nature of human life. Moreover, since this dynamic motion often follows patterns and forms cycles, it constitutes a drama. The simple cycle of a love relationship is the most obvious example of a drama in which we all participate. Every relationship periodically moves from a state of joy to one of frustration, followed by anger and argument, resolution, and a return to joy.

The dramatic element is the most challenging aspect of dialogue because we are caught within it. Within the realm of ideas and reason we may be able to ascend to a greater objectivity, but at the same time we are mortal beings existing within this living drama. In this chapter we consider the nature of the dynamics of this human drama so that we can better understand the nature of the challenge. And we look in general terms at the drama and then consider it in more specific contexts in the following chapters.

The Greek Vision of the Human Drama— Fate and Providence

At the center of the human drama are two principles, *Fate* and *Providence.* These two principles constitute the shape of the Greek's penetrating vision of human life. For the Greeks these two terms are understood in a different way than they are ordinarily understood in English (Fate and Providence are a translation of the Greek terms *Heiromene* and *Pronoia.*). Fate is the power that binds all phenomena in the natural world to their orderly patterns, and Providence is the power that establishes those patterns for the good of the cosmos. In other words, Providence is the cause of Fate. In the human realm, Fate is the principle that determines our lives and our limits. Providence is the power that provides us with the insight to liberate ourselves from these limitations.

The ancient Greek philosophy is not a belief system; it is a vision of life. One does not believe these doctrines on faith. They are expressions of an understanding of a dynamic part of human life that each of us is able to experience directly. It is because the ancients experienced these forces that they established their philosophy. Whatever your view of life, in this chapter you will see the usefulness of these ideas in reflecting upon your life. We first consider these principles in more detail and then in a practical example.

All things in nature are bound by their natural cycles —the waves of the ocean in their ebb and flow and their intimate connection with the moon, the cycle of the seasons, birth and death. Everything in the natural world follows regular patterns and cycles. These patterns establish the limits of nature. Exhalation follows inhalation, waking follows sleeping, death follows birth, and digestion follows eating; each is tied together, and one cannot exist without the other. Because these definite relationships exist, as in the case of life and death, we are able to recognize order in our universe; since there is order and regularity, we are able to predict events in nature. We may not know exactly when death will come, but we can be sure it will, because nothing in the realm of the mortal can escape beyond these bounds. (If there is something that is free from these bounds, then, according to the Greek philosophers, it is not mortal.) Furthermore, the more accurate our observation and understanding of these patterns, the better and more accurately we can predict natural phenomena.

The examples we have so far considered are all primarily physical phenomena, but Fate governs that incorporeal (i.e., non-physical) world of the psyche. The psyche is what the Greeks called the mind, that part of us which orders and directs our individual lives and communes with our particular thoughts, experiences, and dreams. This part of us is not accessible to the senses, and unlike all other experience, our mental or psychic life is not open to the direct experience of others (except perhaps through some kind of supernatural power like telepathy). For this reason the psyche is said to be incorporeal.

In the realm of the psyche there also exist limits and patterns and regular cycles. For example, just as a seed sprung from a tree grows to maturity to be a tree itself, so also human offspring become very much like their parents. And so the old saying goes "The fruit doesn't fall very far from the tree." This is an expression of the limitations of fated existence. Children necessarily become like their parents, no matter how much they wish to prevent this from happening. Although we may at first rebel, eventually we settle into the ways and values of our parents. Although the way in which we settle into the model of our parents may not always be obvious, the settling itself inevitably takes place. For example, one may be the child of a parent who is a religious fundamentalist. When such a child becomes an adult, he may reject religion altogether. In this respect he might believe that he has freed himself from his parent's ways. However, instead of becoming a religious zealot, he has become a political one. In this respect, he has followed the model of his parent in a different area of life and so is not the *same* as the parent but is profoundly *similar*.

In contemporary science many hold to the view that children are genetically predetermined by the workings of physical biology. Although this must be recognized to be an important factor affecting the limitations and boundaries of human life, according to the Greeks it is not the primary factor. It is not the blind workings of a mechanistic universe that determine our lives; it is the function of a metaphysical power called Fate that expresses itself through scientific laws. Fate defines the different gifts and talents, likes and dislikes, and specific inclinations that determine what each person will and will not seek out in life.

The key difference between the mechanistic view and the Greek vision is this. Science does not allow room for the possibility of the liberation from the predispositions of our physical nature. The Greeks do, and they attribute this capacity for liberation to the power of Providence. Liberation from Fate is possible because human beings share in a mortal and immortal nature, that is, a physical and non-physical life. This non-physical part of our life is intelligent and able to participate in the gift of insight that Providence bestows. It is through this kind of insight that we are able to redirect our lives away from their conditioned or determined ends and toward higher and more excellent ones.

This philosophical picture of the cosmos is one that is eminently just. The very workings of Fate are said to be determined by Providence, and in this way everything in the cosmos is ordered for the highest good. The challenge, of course, is to be able to see that the particular events of your life are for your benefit and growth. The discussion in this book aims to contribute to this goal. In the *Republic*, Plato presents a myth to account for the justice of each particular individual's fate. According to the myth of Er, the human soul is immortal and lives through a series of reincarnations. In this story it is described how each individual chooses his or her particular fate based upon the education and nurturing of the soul in its previous incarnation. Consequently, each fate is just, since each individual chooses it freely.

The existence and power of the functioning of Fate (the binding power) can be recognized if you direct your attention to the patterns and cycles of the drama of your life. For each person, in each relationship, and in each family, there exist these patterns and cycles. Although they may not be apparent to those who are attentive only to particular events, they reveal themselves to the mind when one looks out on the course of one's life over a longer period of time. These patterns then emerge clearly, as if you were standing on some marked vista looking out upon a range of mountains. On the other hand, when we examine particulars—single events— it is impossible to see the pattern because it is formed from a sequence of events. Moreover, this kind of seeing demands that you gain a degree of objectivity in your life, which is often a great challenge. It is always easier to recognize the patterns and cycles of another, but we must admit that if they exist for others, they also exist within our own lives.

Fate, Providence, and Relationships—An Example

The nature of Fate and Providence and their functioning in human life can be seen very clearly in relationships. Imagine two people in a relationship. They could be friends, family members, lovers, or co-workers. Let us take the example of two co-workers, Michelle and Bob. Imagine that Michelle is working on a computer and she loses a file. Bob suggests that she reset the computer, go to the backup file, and then start again. Michelle rejects the suggestion out of hand and sets out to try to figure out how to retrieve the file. She asks Bob for help, and he refuses because he feels that Michelle has been disrespectful of him. He supposes that Michelle is thinking that he is a know-it-all. Michelle, on the other hand, does not think he is a know-it-all and wonders why Bob is now distant and is refusing to help. If they have been working together for some time, they will probably notice that this same pattern repeats itself quite often:

1. Bob makes a suggestion.
2. Michelle rejects it out of hand.
3. Bob gets mad and resists continuing the discussion. He thinks Michelle is being disrespectful of him and believes him to be a know-it-all.
4. Michelle wonders why Bob is distant and concludes that Bob thinks she is stupid.
5. This situation creates a tension in the office that lingers.
6. The tension is finally resolved when a friendly scene takes place at the office and the quarrel is forgotten.

The interesting point about our case study is that both Bob and Michelle are completely deluded in their perceptions about the motives and attitude of the other. Michelle does not consider Bob a know-it-all, and Bob does not think that Michelle is stupid. Both are deceived about the reality of the situation. All the same, the two are bound to this little drama. It frustrates and angers each of them and hinders their working relationship. Despite the minor nature of the event, it has the power to reverberate in their minds. Michelle is angered that her co-worker considers her stupid. Bob, on the other hand, feels that Michelle is not respectful of him. He also feels as if he can't get through to her. And he hates being considered a know-it-all when he is trying to help. Both take their frustration and thoughts about the situation home with them. The tension of the relationship is not resolved until a friendly exchange takes place between them. Inevitably, however, a similar frustrating event occurs, and the pattern repeats itself.

Each of us plays out such scenes in our lives on a regular basis. We consistently misinterpret the actions, words, intentions, and states of mind of others and consequently react in a way that is utterly inappropriate. Sometimes this happens for one person, but just as often it happens between two or more people simultaneously. Since this pattern habitually repeats itself and goes through predictable steps or stages (and includes similar thoughts and states of mind), we can attribute it to the power in nature called Fate. This drama establishes the cycles of our relationships, binds us to a way of relating that is less than ideal, and so limits us from achieving greater excellence, freedom, and harmony in our relationships.

The working of Fate makes these cycles predictable and inevitable, but it does not exclude the possibility of growth. Whereas the physical world is bound to these cycles, the human being is not, because humans participate in something beyond physical laws, namely, the power of understanding. Humans can seek to understand the nature of their limited patterns and the truth of their delusions. When this happens, it is attributed to the power of Providence. Providence is the principle in the cosmos that accounts for whatever leads to our liberation from Fate in any degree, small or large. Let us continue with our example.

Imagine, after this drama plays itself out, that Bob decides, rather than to withdraw, to ask Michelle, "Why aren't you going to try my suggestion? It may save you a lot of time. I notice that you always reject my suggestions out of hand, but in the end you follow them anyway. But you always reject my role in helping. Why is that?" Bob's sincerity gently stirs Michelle to an openness where she reveals herself. "When you make a suggestion, it feels to me as though I have to follow it. I feel as if I have to reject it to preserve the individual integrity of my decision-making." Bob is stunned and responds, "And I always thought it was because you didn't like me and were being unfriendly to me. I took it personally when it had nothing to do with me. Wow, that's a relief."

What stirs Bob to inquire rather than to continue being withdrawn and angry? He may have repeated this pattern hundreds or thousands of times with people in his life, and yet in this instance he decides to awaken from the limiting power of his anger and inquire about the truth; this allows him to see his delusion about the nature of the event. Whatever power in the cosmos is responsible for that change in Bob is called Providence. It is called Providence because it liberates humans from the patterns that bind them to a lower kind of life, and this liberation is achieved through a clarity of mind free of anger or other emotions. At the same time,

Michelle also responds positively to Bob's question and reveals her feelings, so that the truth of the matter can be understood. When this kind of clarity and curiosity about the truth is sought, Bob and Michelle discover a genuine understanding of what is really going on. This then compels them to reflect about why they both continually misinterpret each other in these repeated scenes and why such scenes play a big part in their lives. If they pursue this question sincerely, they will each come to see that they play out this pattern with many people in their lives in many and various ways. Moreover, they will see that this drama played itself out in their families, between their parents or their guardians, or between themselves and their parents, or both. Through reflection and questioning, they can discover the reasons why the family engages in such drama, and they can discover the significance it has and how they themselves have taken on the beliefs and ways of being that have bound them to these roles. Through this kind of understanding, they can gain freedom from these limiting dramas.

Tragedy and the Tragic Hero

This is the essence of the Greek view of human drama. There are certain repeated dramas or "games" that families repeatedly play out and that function as a kind of initiation ritual in which the children take on the family's false beliefs and the accompanying roles that determine how they will act. Oftentimes we play out both roles in the drama, but we also enter into situations where we are able to project one of the roles upon someone else. Sometimes two people can be caught up in their own personal dramas simultaneously and thus relate with one another in a way that satisfies each person's particular drama at the same time, even though each drama is different. In other words, although they are different dramas, they can interlock and mesh. Fortunately, there is a power of understanding that lifts us out of this lesser way of being and allows us to free ourselves from these dramas and their delusions.

In Greek philosophy, Providence is a source of goodness in the cosmos that actually governs Fate, so that even though Fate is limiting us in one sense, ultimately, the very function of Fate is for our good, since it serves a beneficial purpose in our lives. If we didn't experience pain or suffering, a negative state resulting from these dramas, we would never want to free ourselves and seek out the power of Providence. Thus, when one experiences this kind of event in one's life, it opens up the possibility of seeing life in a wholly new way, because suddenly there is the awareness that what one thinks is true about a scene may not be true at all. There is also the realization that if we could be so deluded in one set of circumstances, it is very possible that we could be similarly deluded at another time. For in our delusion we have no idea we are deluded. It seems to us that things are exactly as they appear to be, just as Bob and Michelle did not know the truth of their situation. Such an experience gives one an entirely new perspective on life, the recognition that there exist two entirely different ways of being—one in the realm of Fate and one in the realm of the clarity and light of Providence. (In different cultures this same idea is expressed in various ways. In Taoist thought, Fate and Providence are one of the primary meanings of yin and yang, and in Hinduism and Buddhism they are delusion in karmic existence and awakening.)

The central issue that faces humans in life is how to liberate themselves from the confining limits of their fated existence so that they can enjoy the benefit that Providence brings in the clarity of insight and the freedom from one's personal problems. As we mentioned earlier, the dynamics of Providence and Fate constitute the essence of Greek tragedy. When one is caught within the limits of fated existence, one is blocked from seeing the truth of events in one's life and therefore blocked from making the appropriate decisions. The most well-known example of such a tragic figure is Oedipus, the son of the King of Thebes. Upon his birth there is a prophecy that Oedipus will slay his father, King Laius. His father chooses to have him taken to the hills and left to die. Instead, he is saved and raised by a shepherd and later in life hears the prophecy that he will kill his father and marry his mother. He then goes on to unknowingly fulfill the prophecy.

Although this is Oedipus's fate, in the Greek view it does not mean that it is his inevitable and inexorable course in life. Fate is the direction in which the nature of one's existence is leading. All the forces and influences in Oedipus's particular life are pointing him to this end. But even though the course of fate is taking him down this path, it does not mean that he, or any other human being, has no power to wake up to the nature of his fate and alter it. It is as if we are journeying down a mountain path, pulled down by the inertial force of gravity. As we travel down the path, it may become steeper and steeper and the momentum greater and greater. The path may seem to be the necessary one to follow, yet there are always signs along the path indicating where it is leading. It takes clarity of mind to see those signs and courage and wisdom to turn aside and choose an unknown road. In the case of Oedipus, after he receives the prophecy, he immediately goes on to kill an unknown man on the road, who, of course, turns out to be his father. Not long after he arrived at Thebes and is crowned king, he marries an older woman who, in truth, is his own mother. We can only wonder why someone who had heard such a prophecy as Oedipus had would put himself directly in the situation to fulfill the prophecy. The god then sends a plague upon Thebes, which will not be lifted until the murderer of Laius, Oedipus's father, is found. Oedipus, however, seeks throughout the city for the culprit, when he himself is responsible—a fact that he denies. Oedipus is blocked from looking honestly at his own life and seeing the truth, and instead looks for an external cause.

The tragic figure is the individual who ignores signs and refuses to recognize his fate and the bad end to which it is leading. Yet the nature of life is just. In the Greek view, we choose our particular course in life, are provided with opportunities for achieving our highest and most meaningful goals, and are given signs to avoid personal tragedy. The very nature of tragedy is the way in which the cosmos reveals our personal limitations, that is, the limitations of our vision about our personal lives, and life in general. And so the ultimate goal of tragedy is to provide an opportunity for learning, because it is often necessary for us to see fully and explicitly the consequences of our problems before we are willing to change.

Why is this? Why must humans reach tragic ends before being willing to change? Why do we cling to our fated existence in the face of the evidence that it is leading us to harm, whether in small ways or great? In the view of the Greeks, it is a very simple matter. It is not the work of a devil. Nor is it the consequence of genetics or evolutionary biology. It is not the result of emotional trauma or the work of unexplainable forces in the subconscious. Our limitations and fate are simply the consequence of holding on to false beliefs about the nature of ourselves and reality. In other words, they are the outcome of accepting false beliefs as true—thinking one knows when one doesn't know.

What follows from this outlook is a remarkably positive view of the human capacity for change. Contrast this with other pictures of the human situation. One traditional view common to Christianity and other religions is that there exists a war in the universe between forces of good and evil. If human problems are the work of a devil, or some malicious force in the universe, it follows that human growth is always subservient to the nature of this cosmic conflict, a conflict in which mortals are faced with an eternal struggle that their nature is not perfectly fit to take on. In this mythology the possibility of human growth is limited by the power of the evil force that these traditions suppose to exist.

If we consider the more modern view that one's individual situation is determined in large part by genetics and evolutionary biology, a similar dilemma remains. Humans are restricted by their particular physical condition, and this physical limit is insurmountable. Psychology, on the other hand, gives a view similar to the religious picture. Traditionally, it suggests that there is a conflict within human beings, in which they must contend with their rival inner "drives" or "forces." These forces are especially constraining since they are considered to be unconscious. There are also psychological views that claim humans are shaped by emotional experiences that leave permanent "wounds" to one's personality or soul. Such emotional wounds, therefore, restrict one's growth and are never fully healed, and restrict one's growth And there are other views that state that humans are driven by subconscious forces, which must necessarily hamper us, since we are not conscious of them.

The Greek view offers humankind the greatest hope for change, growth, and freedom, because it claims that there are no restrictions upon our growth beyond our own beliefs about our individual lives and our world. Humans choose their particular fate and are therefore free to see their limitations and transcend them; moreover, everything in the cosmos is ordered in such a way as to assist those who seek out this goal, and there exists no physical, emotional, or psychological hindrance to personal or spiritual growth. Each human is considered to have special gifts and a special destiny, and the object of life is to grow beyond the limits of one's fate and seek out this more ideal existence. The very power of the Greek vision is demonstrated by the great achievements of the classical Greek world, which cultivated the greatest excellence in every aspect of human life—visual arts, poetry, statesmanship, science, music, drama, poetry, architecture, athletics, and philosophy.

In pursuit of this supreme goal of life—to transcend Fate and achieve one's destiny—dialogue serves the highest function. It is in dialogue with others that we are able to test our own opinions and discover whether they can stand such evaluation. To enter this process of reflection requires that one be willing to recognize the possibility of being wrong. Oedipus was a king of a great city, and such powerful people as kings are often those least likely to submit to a critical discussion or evaluation of their opinions; these people became the archetypal tragic heroes for the Greek dramatists. In their lives and pursuit of power and greatness, they also acquired great tenacity and stubbornness, and few were in a position to challenge them for fear of their wrath. But when they were challenged by seers, companions, or family members, they were unable to let go of what they thought they knew to be true, and consequently failed to gain the beneficent insight bestowed by Providence that would have freed them and their cities from the tragic ends they met.

Philosophy and the Human Drama

The dramatists did not deal with the problems posed by their works. They merely portrayed the archetypal ways in which heroes confronted their fates. It became the domain of philosophy, and especially Socratic dialectic, to investigate the way in which people cling to what they think they know. Socrates' entire life was devoted to challenging the claims of those who thought they knew. He saw himself as providing an invaluable service to his city. By his thorough manner of testing, people were able to discover whether they indeed did know, and if one did know, then such knowledge could be shared in the city. However, if one was shown not to know, then he would be compelled through rational argument to abandon his beliefs; in this way, the community would be liberated from whatever harm might occur by virtue of such individuals functioning with their false beliefs, sharing them with others, or passing them on to their children.

As one might imagine, those powerful figures in the city who thought they knew, but were shown by Socrates not to know, often did not accept it gracefully. Although the reasoning of the dialogue led to the clear conclusion that their own opinions were false, many were unable to accept what reasoning demonstrated. Faced with evidence that the central beliefs in their lives were false they were put in a severe crisis. It is likely that those false convictions were passed down by parents, religious authorities, and the community. No doubt these people closely identified with their beliefs, which formed the basis of their relationships with friends and family. Few individuals are willing to let go of these cherished attachments. Instead the elite of the city charged Socrates with being a sorcerer with words, one who cleverly used logic to deceive others into giving up their own opinions.

In such a dialogue, when an individual is faced with seeing the falsity of his or her beliefs, it brings about a phenomenon called "being stung." Imagine what it is like to reach a place where your central beliefs are challenged and appear to be false. The very possibility of having to abandon them causes a crisis. It seems as if the floor beneath your feet has been drawn away. Where can you stand? Beliefs guide your life. How can you live without them? The very possibility of abandoning them leaves you in a state of loss, emptiness, puzzlement, and not knowing. For most, this condition is very disconcerting and unsettling, which is why many in Athens feared Socrates. For it was genuinely recognized that Socrates himself was in such a state—puzzled and not knowing—and that he went on to put others in the same condition. And when one ended up in this state, he or she experienced the shock of being stung. It is expressed this way in *Meno:*

Meno: Socrates, even before I began meeting with you, I used to hear that you are nothing other than a man who is at a loss and who makes others be at a loss, too. And now, as it certainly appears to me, you are bewitching me, placing spells upon me, and completely subduing me with your charms, so that I have become full of being at a loss. If you don't mind a little joke, you appear to me to be exactly like the flat-faced stingray that swims in the sea, both in your appearance and in other ways, for this fish always stings whoever approaches or touches it and makes them numb. And now you appear to have done this same sort of thing to me, because I am really and truly numb in my soul and in my tongue, and I don't have any answer to give you. And yet I have given "thousands" of lengthy speeches on excellence in front of great audiences, and they were especially good, too—so they appeared to me, at least. But now I am not able to say in any way what excellence is. It appears to me that you would be well advised not to take any sea journeys nor even to leave this city, for if you should do the sorts of things you do as a stranger in another city, you would be quickly imprisoned as a sorcerer.

Socrates: You are a rogue, Meno, and you almost took me in.

Meno: What exactly do you mean, Socrates?

Socrates: I recognize why you make this comparison of me.

Meno: Why do you think?

Socrates: So I would make a comparison of you in return. I know this about all handsome and beautiful people—they are gratified by these comparisons, because it profits them. The comparisons made of beauties are always beautiful, but I will not make a comparison of you. As for the one about me, if the stingray makes others numb because it is in a state of numbness itself, then it fits. But if this is not the case, it doesn't. For I don't put others at a loss because I am filled with all the answers, but, in fact, I put others at a loss because I am at a loss. So now concerning what excellence is, I, at least, don't know, but perhaps you did know before you touched me. Now, however, you are only like one who doesn't know; but nonetheless, I am willing to consider and search with you for what, after all, excellence is.

The Issue of Knowing and Not Knowing

In ancient times, as well as today, knowing was of monumental importance. We expect our parents to know how to live and what to do and to be able to answer our questions about life. Our teachers have the responsibility of knowing and imparting their knowledge about the different aspects of the world to us. We rely on professionals, like doctors and psychologists, expecting them to know how to heal our minds and bodies. We depend upon experts to give us knowledge about what is good for us and our society. We turn to religious leaders for knowledge about the ultimate questions of life. And we support those political leaders who we believe really know how to improve our country.

In our own lives, as well, we are expected to know. When we are children, our parents expect us to know what is wrong and right. Our teachers want us to demonstrate what we have learned from our studies and have gained in knowledge. We are tested regularly for twelve to twenty years to ensure that we become expert knowers about the facts of grammar, history, science, and so on. Those who are not able to demonstrate this knowing are punished with bad grades. Upon finishing one's studies of these general subjects, we are expected to go on to a field of specialty ourselves and become expert knowers who can be called upon by businesses or individuals to help society function. And, in turn, we become parents and pass on our knowledge and wisdom to our children.

Conversely, consider what it is like when we don't know something we are supposed to know. It is often embarrassing—we feel stupid or ignorant. It can also be extremely painful—we feel badly about ourselves and grow depressed, low in spirit. Yet, on the other hand, when we do know (or at least think we know) we revel in it. We are filled with life; we are confident, proud, and joyful and take on a positive image of ourselves. We are literally trained to be knowers and to look upon not knowing as a dreadful and fearful state, something about which one should be embarrassed, a state considered to be extremely dangerous. And so it is no wonder that when given the choice between appearing to be a knower or a not knower, we often choose the former even when the truth is that we really don't know. We hide our not knowing behind the mask of knowing. As a common phrase admonishes, "Don't show your ignorance."

Of course, there are many situations in which a certain kind of knowledge is essential. It would not be a good thing to go to a dentist who was not trained and certified in the knowledge of filling cavities. Nor would it be right for a pilot to fly a plane without the knowledge of aviation. Most of the important functions in our society require what we call "skills." These skills are the things we go to school to learn or gain from work experience. The problem with "knowing," however, is that it sets a limit on our vision. This limitation is expressed beautifully in a famous talk given by Suzuki Roshi: "In the beginner's mind there are many possibilities, but in the expert's there are few."*

For example, although doctors of medicine gain much so-called knowledge, there are a large number of cases that they are unable to effectively treat. The same is true of professional therapists. Studies have shown that a professional, with all his or her knowledge, is no more effective in counseling than a well-intentioned college-educated person. Degrees, however, present an image of knowing, and when one takes on such an image, he or she is much more unlikely to reveal those instances when they don't know. Many doctors, for example, hold to this image of knowing what is the best

---

*Shunryu Suzuki, *Zen Mind, Beginner's Mind* (New York: Weatherhill, 1986), p. 21.

course for a patient when they have only an opinion based on a certain degree of evidence, which is far from knowledge. The truth is that there is always the chance that they might be wrong. There is always a possibility of a mistake in diagnosis. Humans are fallible, and the human understanding of the body and the nature of health is limited. In the strict sense of the term, doctors never know what is best for their patients. They merely have an opinion based on a certain degree of understanding. The same can be said for any professional in any context. This kind of analysis is not skepticism with all its negative connotations, but rather the rational recognition of the inherent fallibility of mortal creatures. It does not reject understanding and reason and the need for science and fields of knowledge. What it proclaims is the danger of putting on a false appearance of knowing when one really does not know.

When one claims to know anything in an absolute way, one is false to the nature of the situation. The appearance of knowing is very reassuring. Reality and its accompanying uncertainty are much more troublesome, which is why we often look to those who are able to convince us of their knowing by a bold, confident, and assuring state of mind. However, when one's claim to knowing becomes absolute and final, it closes off completely the consideration of other possibilities and the need for dialogue.

While knowing is considered in such a positive light and not knowing with such negative connotations, it is quite often just the opposite. A state of knowing is often presented behind a false appearance that cuts off questioning, investigation, and inquiry. Not knowing, on the other hand, is most often a state of sincerity, honesty, and openness that allows for wonder, puzzlement, mystery, and questioning. It is the prerequisite for inquiry and investigation. It sets no limits but preserves the need for exploration. It cultivates tolerance and friendliness. It is free of any prejudice. It is the natural state of children—and even fills adults with a childlike wonder and enjoyment for learning which results in vitality. It allows for spontaneity and appropriate action in the moment because it preserves a clear and free state of mind. Most importantly, not knowing is the very condition for insight and growth.

It is for these reasons that Socrates entered into dialogue with others—to seek to discover when he thought he knew but did not know. Socrates recognized the danger of this state—sometimes called "double ignorance"—of thinking one knows when one doesn't know. Many in Athens did not understand this concept and believed Socrates to be nothing more than another clever Sophist who enjoyed proving others wrong. They did not appreciate the valuable service that Socrates sought to provide his fellow citizens. In the dialogue *Charmides*, his friend Critias makes an accusation against him:

Critias: I believe you are doing the very thing you denied you were doing just now: for you are attempting to refute me, without troubling to follow the subject of our discussion.

Socrates: How can you think, if my main effort is to refute you, that I do it with any other motive than that which would impel me to investigate the meaning of my own words—from a fear of carelessly supposing, at any moment, that I knew something while I knew it not? And so it is now: that is what I am doing, I tell you. I am examining the argument mainly for my own sake but also, perhaps, for that of my other intimates. Or do you not think it is for the common good, almost of all men, that the truth about everything there is should be discovered?

Critias: Yes, indeed, I do, Socrates.

Socrates: Then take heart, I say, my admirable friend, and answer the question put to you as you deem the case to be, without caring a jot whether it is Critias or Socrates who is being refuted. Give the argument itself your attention, and observe what will become of it under the test of reasoning.

Dialogue and the Human Drama

The essence of the drama of human life is simple. To some degree we are all blocked from seeing our lives as they really are but instead get caught up in our false perceptions of events and words. These false perceptions are projected from the internal drama of our own psyches and are based on what we think we know about our own lives and the world, which, in turn, generates the roles and masks we wear as we present what we think we know. Dialogue is the activity that draws out this drama, because it invites us to characterize what we think we know in words. And so dialogue provides the best opportunity for us to see our false beliefs and perceptions. Dialogue is the arena for this drama, and we enter it with others. In dialogue we are faced not only with the challenge of considering the issue at hand but also with the possibility of our own false projections, our partner's false projections, and the drama produced as a result of the interaction of these projections and the content of the dialogue.

Given the challenge of the human drama in which we all participate, it is our next task to consider how we can best function within a dialogue. Since there is going to be drama in every dialogue, we benefit when we commit to an objective approach, such as the one outlined in this book. When dialogists are committed to a standard for their dialogic relationship, it becomes an objective means of judging one's participation in the relationship. Whenever emotions, attitudes, or difficulties arise in the dialogue, the dialogists can always refer back to the principles and the structure that are governing their interchange. Neither party need feel that the dialogue is being controlled by another; it is ruled by a shared and accepted guideline for proceeding. An important part of that standard is how we treat one another, and dialogists must commit to the highest ideals of human friendship. Dialogue is about relating to one another and demands a high degree of care and trust for the other and a profound respect for the human mind, as well as for each individual person's mind.

In spite of all attempts to maintain objectivity, there are clearly going to be times when people become angry, frustrated, enraged, hurt, and so forth. Human beings are not logical computers that have no emotional connection to their opinions. We are living, caring, feeling creatures, and so we have strong feelings about what we think to be true and have invested feelings in what we consider to be false; when we enter into a discussion of these matters, these feelings naturally arise, and we ought not to suppress them (though, depending on the context, it may be appropriate to moderate the expression of them). The very fact that we do have these responses reveals something about our humanness. We not only think about the world but, through emotions, we also demonstrate to others how we feel about the world. We will never rid ourselves of emotions, nor would we want to, but we need to consider their effect on our goal of dialogue.

A dialogue is a rational procedure for exploring an issue and seeking the truth. Emotions are those states that emerge from ourselves when we consider different thoughts. They literally "move outward" from us, for that is what emotion means, and so they have the power to move us and others. Emotions can be a strong force to persuade others to do what we wish them to do. Yet when we appeal to this element in others, we attempt to bypass the reasoning and evaluative part of a person's mind, and that is an unfriendly means of persuasion because it is a form of control. Through reason, friends seek to discover the truth together and follow a shared and agreed-upon path, having come to one mind about the issue. Emotions also have the power to distract us from a balanced and fair evaluation of an issue. When we are in the grip of a strong emotion, such as anger, it is very difficult, if not impossible, to preserve the clarity needed to see the truth of what is being said and what is taking place. Very often an emotional response is the doorway to taking on one of the roles from the dramas we play out in our lives, and we ought to be very attentive to the stirrings of such emotions. Thus, it is essential in dialogue to cultivate a quality which the Greeks called *sophrosyne*, which means keeping one's temper or, literally, saving one's mind.

Dialogists must train themselves to be attentive to their own states of mind as well as the states of those with whom they are engaging in dialogue. The ideal state of mind for dialogue is one in which we are completely objective, clear-thinking, and unaffected by emotions, but as humans we are easily thrown off the track. One ought not to hide this fact and put on a mask of objectivity when one is really angry or stirred by a certain position. To do this is to be untrue to one's state of mind, presenting a false appearance to our dialogic partner. This insincerity detracts from the integrity of a dialogue and undermines the trust and honest relationship that dialogists seek to establish. Instead, it is much more beneficial to attempt to reveal one's emotions and to express them in words. This has a number of beneficial effects. First off, it releases the power of the emotions, since they, by their very nature, seek to be expressed. When they are buried or held on to, they only gain in power over our coolheadedness. Secondly, when emotions are expressed and articulated clearly in words, we are better able to objectively evaluate a state of mind. As a result the emotional state gains a kind of existence in the world that allows us to look at it and separate ourselves from it, so that we can then evaluate if the emotion is appropriate or helpful for the dialogue. Most often, the emotion is the result of a certain belief or position, and once the emotion is articulated the dialogist can have the opportunity to express the reason for the emotion and make that a part of the dialogue. For this reason, dialogists should encourage their partners to articulate their emotions, if they believe a strong emotion is present.

States of mind also reveal where an individual stands with respect to the position being discussed. The primary goal of dialogue is to engage the other on the most honest and sincere level. A state of mind often reveals whether a dialogist is being truly open and giving her genuine position. Often people speak from what they have heard others say or what they believe they are expected to say. If one suspects that to be the case, one can inquire if the person genuinely holds that position. A dialogist may also take a position just to try to refute the other. This is also not sincere, and one has a right to question a person about her motives in the dialogue.

The entire range of the human drama enters the arena of dialogue and offers the dialogist a great challenge. Although it is ideal to be as open and sincere as possible in one's expression and discussion of ideas, there is also another factor that must be considered for effective communication, namely, timing. As in every activity, timing is a central issue. One ought not to function in a dialogue according to mechanical rules, following the logic and reasoning of the discussion blindly. There are often times when the subject is very personal in nature and quite challenging to the people engaged in the exploration. If there are certain issues that are clearly very sensitive to one's partner, issues that raise the individual's blocks or prejudices, then it demands great skill and insight to know how to introduce and explore them properly. Clearly, in such cases, the dialogists must establish a good dialogic relationship, where they trust each other and are able to be open and honest. If such a relationship is established, these issues should arise as a natural part of the dialogue and in their appropriate place. And if one party is put into a crisis over the issue, it is pertinent to raise that state of mind for discussion, since it blocks the dialogue from continuing.

There are necessarily going to be times when people in a dialogue are thrown into a personal crisis and may completely lose their tempers. This possibility must be recognized and accepted; it is not something that should be avoided. It is often the case that humans must face such a crisis in order to fully see the implications of their beliefs. And there are many beliefs that have a terribly strong hold on the psyche and that are protected by these kinds of emotional defenses. Individuals may avoid vital dialogues and prevent others from inviting such dialogues by means of these strong emotional responses. We ought not to be put off by such defenses in ourselves or others. At the same time, a dialogist's goal should not be to spark this kind of crisis in another. It must merely be something that accompanies a natural and reasonable discussion.

Yin and Yang Principles

In dealing with the issue of emotions, it may be helpful to consider the Chinese yin and yang theory. Yin and yang are two principles that manifest in every aspect of nature. They can be considered the principles that define the movement and structure of the natural world and therefore our fated existence. Yin is the principle of the withdrawal of energy, and yang is the manifestation and expression of energy. A few examples of this relationship will explain the distinction. Inhalation is an expression of yin, exhalation of yang; sleeping is yin, waking life is yang; the ebb of a wave is yin, and the flow is yang; the feminine aspect of nature is yin, and the masculine is yang. Accordingly, we can see that everything in nature is in a constant state of motion between these two principles, and one is taught the nature of yin and yang so that one can recognize this motion and deal with particular situations accordingly.

We can also recognize this balance in dialogue. A dialogue is an exchange of ideas between two people. There are two roles—those of questioner and answerer—and with every interchange each person must take her turn as speaker and listener. The speaker is yang, and the listener is yin. One of the most difficult tasks in a dialogue is to listen. When listening, we must rest our own thinking process and be open and receptive to the speaker, an archetypal yin quality. Yet we often are stirred by what the other person is saying, and these thoughts become like energy rising within us, seeking to be expressed and set into motion. We must understand that this is not appropriate to the role of listener. The difficulty can be dealt with if we recognize that there is a natural rhythm and harmony between speaker and listener. Just like the even movement of breath between inhalation and exhalation, we must accept that words must be received and taken in before it is appropriate to respond and continue the flow of the dialogue. Conversely, there are also those who are more comfortable in the role of listener because they are hesitant to speak their minds. These people, too, must see that they have a valuable part to play in the dialogue and must participate fully in order for the dialogue to be meaningful and complete.

The idea of yin and yang can also be used to address the issue of states of mind. States of mind ebb and flow just like every other phenomenon in nature. An individual who becomes angry cannot stay angry, and that anger must eventually subside. Of course, the rhythm of emotions is different in each of us. Some people may be able to hold on to anger much more stubbornly than others. In dialogue, one must be attentive to that rhythm. As one encounters the different points along the path of a certain state of mind, there will be different opportunities; however, this depends completely upon the particular situation and person involved. It is very possible that if an individual reaches a peak of anger, it may be the perfect time for him to ask her to look at her state of mind. She may then look at her anger and see how out of place it is. On the other hand, there are other people who this might cause to become more angry and even violent. There are no clear rules for how to handle these situations. If one attempts to deal with someone who is in a crisis and in an extreme emotional state, there is always a risk. At the same time, even these states present opportunities for learning and growth. It demands a high degree of insight and maturity for a dialogist to be effective in such a situation.

When it comes to emotions, we are often in a much better position to deal with our own than someone else's. Before being able to work with others and their dramas, it is essential that we gain an understanding of the nature of our own psychic patterns. The idea of yin and yang can be especially helpful here. We can feel those times when emotions begin to surge within us—the rising of yang—and then when they begin to withdraw—the movement of yin. By examing the dynamics of our inner life, we can better understand it. And, if we see that these states come and go, we can also be better prepared to avoid getting caught up or overtaken by such emotional forces. We can begin to gain a critical distance from this inner drama, and this is the start of the cultivation of *sophrosyne*, which is a most beneficial quality for the activity of dialogue.

Dialogue As a Path to Personal Growth

Dialogue demands the highest human excellence and thus offers us a remarkable opportunity for personal growth. It is an intimate activity in which we are invited to reveal the truth about who we are and how we see the world. Dialogue asks us to put into words what is most significant and meaningful in our lives, an activity that inherently contains risks. For the better part of our lives we are in the interesting position of being able to consider our thoughts and opinions in the privacy of our own minds, where there is no one to see us, no one to judge our flaws or peculiarities, and where we may revel in our fantasies and delusions and take pride in our grandiose self-images. Yet all of these are no more real than a dream.

In dialogue, however, we disclose our thoughts to the world for objective evaluation with others. Whenever we open up and reveal our thoughts, there is always fear and danger concerning what will happen. How will the other respond? Even in this land of freedom, we do not grow up in a culture of free speech. As children, we do not have the freedom to speak our minds. We view the world with a natural wonder and curiosity, free of prejudice and seeing things as they truly are. Few families, however, permit the free expression of this kind of clarity, the kind that challenges the fundamental beliefs and ways of being of the family. Honesty and clarity are a threat to all false appearances and beliefs, and children often see right through these matters but then are silenced. (In this regard, children can take the role of Socrates within the family.)

As we grow older, we are taught so-called propriety, that is, when it is appropriate to speak and when it is not. We certainly do not live in a world where honesty and directness are granted free reign. We learn "politeness" and "respect." But this is just a way of protecting the appearances and the social games of our specific families and communities. As a consequence, we are trained as it were to restrict our speech. For some there exists an internal censor who reviews all prospective thoughts before their journey to communication into words. For others, the monitor has become a tyrant who silences any maverick thought the moment it arises, so that soon enough the individual stops having such thoughts or forgets that they ever arose in the first place.

This is the background for dialogue—we enter the grounds of dialogue asked to speak boldly, freely, and truthfully, and immediately there arises a terrible fear. Do I want such freedom? What will happen if I speak my mind? How will the other person respond? Will I be hated, scolded, made an outcast, ridiculed, attacked, assaulted, exiled? All of these responses are a very real part of the human drama of dialogue, and they need to be considered seriously. These are the personal blocks to genuine communication and understanding between us and others. The fact is that to enter into dialogue demands *courage*. When we reveal ourselves, we enter into the unknown. We don't know how our words will be taken. Thus, it is very important to establish a good understanding of the nature of dialogue with those whom we choose to engage in dialogue. We have to have a degree of confidence and trust in our partners to enter into this game, or else the plain freedom from fear. Therefore, it is important to establish firm ground upon which to discuss one's concerns and to understand the nature of the game being entered into. A good way to begin is simply to put one's concerns into words, for this is the first step in revealing oneself.

Dialogue demands that we call forth out of ourselves the highest human qualities. As was said earlier, it demands the courage to enter into the unknown. Many feel they have to wait to gain the courage to act, which, may lead to a vicious cycle. "I don't have the courage to reveal myself, so I can't enter into a dialogue." However, this is not the nature of courage. Courage is not a commodity that one simply receives in life; it is an energy that one gains in action. When we recognize that there is a worthy goal and that the goal is accompanied by risk, courage is the awareness that we must face the unknown and that it is a more honorable and noble path than resting in one's fear and not taking the first step. Courage does not dissolve fear. It provides the energy for facing fear in the recognition that it is noble and worthwhile to face it. It is the means to take on a challenge that enables us to grow and transcend the psychic boundaries that limit us. Courage is distinguished by philosophers from boldness, which is the willingness to blindly enter into a dangerous situation. It is not courage to blindly enter a dangerous situation. It is courageous to face a fearful situation, trusting in the opportunity for good that it offers.

Because fear and risk are present in dialogue, it is essential for dialogists to treat one another with the greatest *fairness*. We must be conscious of the difficulty of this endeavor. We need to treat others with the greatest respect and *friendliness* and be concerned for their well-being and development. When a person decides to take the risk of revealing himself and expresses his fear, we must acknowledge the significance of that. Moreover, we cannot demand that those who are fearful go further in a dialogue than they are prepared to go. The building of trust and confidence takes time.

Dialogue also demands the greatest *honesty*. When we refuse to communicate our true thoughts and hide behind a false appearance, we sabotage the integrity of the dialogue. If we are not prepared to reveal ourselves in the dialogue, then it is our responsibility to make this known. At that point, our partner may request that the fear itself become a subject of dialogue, and that can be an important thing to explore. It is, of course, the individual's choice whether to proceed with such a discussion.

In dialogue we are often confronted with positions and opinions we find outrageous, plain wrong, even stupid, and yet it is the responsibility of dialogists to seek to explore such positions and opinions fairly and objectively, no matter what their personal views. This requires the quality we discussed earlier called *sophrosyne*, which means "keeping one's cool." This doesn't mean that we ought to put on a false pretense of objectivity when we are not objective. At any time we feel a strong emotion, it is helpful to express it. We could say, "I have often heard that opinion, and honestly it outrages me. I would like to be able to evaluate it fairly without prejudging it or becoming emotional, yet at the same time it might be difficult for me." In this way we let our partner know where we stand; the dialogists can then proceed together along the path of dialogue—whether they agree or disagree initially about the position being explored.

When we are both courageous and sincere in dialogue, we are able to enter the activity fully and in a state of not knowing. This state is the principal condition for growth, for it signifies that we have journeyed beyond our limitations. It is only when we venture forth beyond these limitations that we can discover the qualities and abilities to function on a higher level in whatever we do. It is at this moment that we have the opportunity for fundamental insight into our lives and our capacities. Our growth, therefore, is necessarily proportional to our willingness to enter into this state of not knowing.

Independently of any particular insight we may gain into an issue through dialogue, from what has been discussed in this chapter it follows that the very qualities required for the activity of dialogue necessarily will benefit us. Courage, keeping one's cool, fairness, friendliness, and honesty are all virtues that when practiced make us better human beings. Moreover, each of these qualities prepares us for the clarity needed to help discover that truth which is being sought. Whatever power leads us to see the truth is called wisdom, and so these virtues are the precondition for our inner wisdom to emerge, and with its emergence we may receive and share the benefit of a clear vision of the truth.

6 THE INNER DIALOGUE

The True Voice

Perhaps the most important dialogues we shall ever have are with ourselves. These dialogues determine our very lives and actions, and, in light of this, it is essential that we discuss the nature of the inner dialogue. Inner dialogues raise a curious question—who are the dialogists? We are each an individual person, and yet we live with a multitude of different inner voices speaking out and addressing us—voices which can be friendly, argumentative, sarcastic, helpful and benevolent, or even malevolent and harmful. And they are as diverse as the voices we hear in our everyday world. With so many voices being heard, it is natural to ask: *Which one is my own? Of all these voices, which expresses my genuine and true self?*

Those who practice Zen, or other forms of meditation, offer helpful insight into this question. In the Zen tradition there is a practice of intensive meditation called *seshin*. The Japanese word *seshin* means to "unify," and this is the very point of the practice. During *seshin*, Zen practitioners devote eight hours to sitting meditation interspersed with formal eating ceremonies, chanting, and periods of work. There is no talking, except when necessary, and throughout the day the practitioner aims to continue the meditation through whatever activity he or she is engaged in. The weeklong *seshin* begins Sunday evening and ends the next Sunday at noon. What is most remarkable is that nearly everyone who practices *seshin* experiences a very similar cycle during that week.

One of the basic elements of Zen is to not follow one's thoughts, as we spoke of earlier. When one turns away from everyday life and enters the *seshin* environment, where one's normal thought patterns are interrupted, the mind usually revolts. For the first few days, it sends out a barrage of thoughts to direct the Zen practitioner off the course. During these first days there may be periods of calm and quiet, but they are interrupted as ordinary thoughts about one's fears, desires, and worries or thoughts about other people arise to interfere with one's practice. At this time, one's mind and thoughts do not play a supportive role, but instead enter the meditation dragging and kicking, so to speak. They also attack the individual, putting him down, casting doubts, and raising all sorts of negative thoughts. (It is also possible to take on a different kind of practice that works to discover why these particular thoughts arise when they do. This is a different, but beneficial practice that will be considered later on.)

But on the third day (sometimes the fourth), there is a major shift. Suddenly that part of the mind that has been hindering the practice gives way, and the individual gains a centeredness and a calm free of distracting thoughts. The mind ceases to fight against itself, and so there is greater unity. With the freedom from these negative thoughts, one experiences a greater vitality. There is also a state of clarity that allows the highest functioning of the mind and helps the Zen student penetrate more deeply into the meditation practice and gain a deeper appreciation and understanding of the nature of existence.

In this state the negative voices sometimes are still heard, but much less often. When they are, they do not have the force they previously had, but instead appear like ripples on a clear pond that softly fade away. One is able to recognize their unreality and weakness. From this state of unity, another voice emerges with greater strength. This voice is soft as well, but it is very calm and clear, possessing great purpose and clear direction; it is broad in its wisdom and warm in its friendliness. It is a voice that encourages one to open up to situations and see what is there; it has great courage and coolheadedness and trust, allowing one to approach situations that are usually disturbing with a fresh, unprejudiced, and objective eye. Of all the voices that fill our heads, this one is certainly not the loudest, but once the scene is cleared so that it can emerge and be recognized, it shows itself as the most wise, friendly, and beneficial voice of the chorus. Since it is a voice that aims to support us, we can call it a voice of wisdom.

What Zen practice shows us is that each of us participates in this kind of wisdom. It is not something special, and in Zen it is called the ordinary mind. However, the nature of our ordinary mind is obscured by all the chatter and emotions that usually fill us. This voice of wisdom rests like a diamond in the rough, waiting to be discovered and brought to light; once it is brought out, it has a natural function that illuminates more brightly when exercised appropriately. Plato calls this part of the soul the reasoning element, and he says that it is the highest and most godlike part of us. It is not merely a logical faculty but is much richer and broader than what we call logic or reason today. It is better to call it the wisdom element in us. Plato does not call it this because to him the reasoning element must be purified and trained to function wisely. The very practice it must take on is the one we have described above— the soul must harmonize its many parts into a unity.

The many individual aspects of the soul reflect its basic needs and functioning. Each of these elements seeks to ensure that its needs are satisfied, and so it possesses a voice through which to express itself. Our need for food and sex and other desires, Plato terms the desiring part of our souls. There is also the need for growth and activity and the expression of life, voiced by the spirited element of the soul. And there is that which seeks the truth, the wisdom or reasoning element. Thus Plato distinguishes three basic divisions of the soul—reason, spirit, and desire. One of the goals of philosophy is to order the soul so that these three work together in their proper relation. Most humans are ruled most often by desire, the lowest element. Others are ruled by spirit. Few are governed by reason. The goal of ancient philosophical practices was for reason to enlist the spirited element in the soul to support its goals and rule over desire. The reason element uses its persuasive ability and enlists the energy of the spirited element to bring the different elements of the soul into a unity, the same way as the three chief notes of a scale come together in the unison of a musical chord. When this is achieved, one kind of wisdom can emerge in us.

The life of the mind is much richer than our contemporary scientific thinking which does not articulate a language for the voices of wisdom. All ancient Wisdom traditions do. In the ancient Greek world the gods and goddesses represented in mythological and symbolic form the different forces that we encounter in our world. The Greeks had a rich symbolic language to represent the life of the psyche and its range of experience and functioning. Many have sought to recapture this language, but those who are intimate with the metaphysical philosophy of the ancient Greeks are aware that the accuracy and profundity of the ancient worldview has barely been tapped.

Socrates, however, challenged the mythological and religious tradition of Athens by introducing the idea of a personal demigod called a *daimon*, which he said spoke to him throughout his life. In Plato's philosophy, each of us is appointed such a guardian spirit, whose responsibility it is to ensure that we follow the course of life that we have chosen, for in the Platonic philosophy we each choose our lives and destinies. In the case of Socrates, this daimon spoke to him from an early age, but according to his account, it never told him what to do but only turned him away from what was not permitted. For Emerson and Thoreau, this voice is our inner genius, and in this age it is referred to as our higher self. Those who are able to build a relationship with this inner voice have benefited greatly.

Paul Brunton's Lessons on Intuition

Paul Brunton gives a wonderful account of the cultivation of these higher faculties of the mind in his classic work, *The Wisdom of the*

Overself. Brunton calls this voice of wisdom within us intuition, and it is the province of this intuition to present us with the wisdom that can turn us away from what is harmful and help guide us toward what is most beneficial. Ordinarily, when we seek to make decisions in our lives, we call upon our thinking mind and go through a consideration of pros and cons. This kind of activity is self-conscious, active, and inquisitive, since we actively consider which is the best path. Intuition, on the other hand, is spontaneous, receptive, and passive.

Each of us has experienced intuition in our lives. For example, when we have been thinking about a question or issue in our lives and then take a break from this process, sometimes from out of nowhere an answer emerges. Brunton calls this spontaneous because it happens suddenly. We are not at that moment seeking the answer; instead we are passive and prepared to receive. Very often this occurs when we awake from a nap or from sleep. There are many famous examples of individuals who have achieved great realizations in mathematics, art, statesmanship, and philosophy in this way.

Yet intuition remains a mystery. When we actively seek the answer, this kind of intuition does not arise. But if we break off the search, it often appears when we least expect it and without our conscious effort. And yet if we hadn't put in the effort in the first place, it is likely that such an intuition would not have come. In those moments when we are no longer actively seeking the answer, what part of the mind is? And why is it that we are not aware of this kind of work going on? Perhaps it is because there *is* no work going on. Instead, what sages tell us is that the highest part of the mind works effortlessly and spontaneously. It is not a matter of working to gain and cultivate this power; it is a matter of preparing ourselves for its reception. This source of intuition cannot be cultivated because it is ever present within us. We must therefore learn the way of communication between this source and our conscious minds. I have resisted using the word *unconscious* to describe this source, as it is often described, because it is clearly conscious of our world. Rather than call it unconscious, it would be more appropriate to call it superconscious. Some also deny that this source is intellect. Clearly, it is not intellect in the sense of the word as it is used in the contemporary world, which limits intellect to logical activity. It is, however, Intellect and Mind in the sense that it is a power for supreme vision of Truth.

According to Brunton there are eight points that must be kept in mind in developing our relationship with the source of intuition.

1) Believe that the answer exists within yourself to be found.

As Socrates says, it is essential to believe that the answer you seek exists for you to be discovered, otherwise you would not seek after it. This belief awakens the desire for the answer, and initiates the energy needed to discover the insight or guidance you are in need of.

2) Direct the full power of your thinking upon the question until you reach a point of complete puzzlement about the issue.

In the next step you cultivate the mind of a Zen student in a one-pointed meditation. Take the question or issue facing you and formulate it in the most precise way you can, then direct the full power of your thinking on concentrating to seek out an answer. This is the most active part of the process. Examine the issue in as many ways as you can, considering all the pertinent information. Talk to yourself and your friends about the issue and then hold the question in your mind until you reach an utter state of puzzlement. The goal is to let your mind be filled as completely as possible with the question and the state of not-knowing. This energizes the mind, allows it to become engrossed in the question, and pushes your thinking until it is at a complete loss. This process can take days or even weeks. (When it comes to the most profound questions, it can take years.)

3) Allow your mind to rest from its active pursuit of the answer.

The active search for an answer prepares the way for intuition, but it can also block its reception. For genuine intuition to arise, you must reach a point at which the energy of the intuitive power can speak and be heard. This can only occur when the deliberating activity of the thinking mind is at rest from its pursuit.

4) Consider the question before taking a nap or going to sleep.

Intuitions often are received upon waking from sleep. During sleep the thinking mind rests and we open up to the intuitive power. A practical means to discovering the intuition is by taking up the question gently before going to bed or taking a nap. As you fall asleep the mind continues to search for the answer. Upon waking, consider the question and see if the answer appears.

5) Develop your sensitivity and receptivity to the subtle communications of your intuition.

Intuitions have a very special quality. They are very much like dreams in that a dream can have remarkable power and depth, but upon waking has the tendency to disappear in an instant. Intuitions, Brunton says, are "as swiftly evanescent and as delicately fragile as is the memory of most dreams after waking up from them." Therefore, it is essential to cultivate one's own sensitivity and receptivity to their subtle communications. Brunton likens this to setting an antennae to a radio signal. By directing one's attention to the subtle communications of the intuition, they will gain in strength and clarity. A very effective means by which to capture these messages is to record your thoughts and dreams in a tape recorder, if possible, or to write them down in a journal.

6) Be patient.

When dealing with the intuitive mind, it is essential to remain patient. Impatience will lead you to accept an impostor for the reality of genuine insight. Intuitions almost always occur when we are not thinking about the question. These impatient urgings block us from entering the state of openness that is necessary for receiving an intuition.

Brunton also points out that intuition may also manifest in forms we might not expect. Answers may come from a line in a book, an image in a movie, or from a dialogue with a friend. Although the intuition may be communicated through an external source, it is a direct response to your seeking.

7) Evaluate alleged intuitions by the strictest standards of your reasoning.

One of the most difficult aspects of intuition is the ability to evaluate a claim to intuitive truth. Often we look toward intuition because ordinary means have failed. We also look to intuition as a source of infallible truth. However, reliance on an internal guide or message is very risky. In order to limit the risk, you should attempt to evaluate the intuition by every means possible. Is it reasonable? Does it conform to the facts of experience? To the degree that it does the risk can be limited.

If an intuition does not conform to the standards of reason and experience, we do enter the realm of risk, but that does not mean the intuition is not accurate. We appeal to intuition in hope of transcending what reason and experience reveal. To minimize the risk of being deceived by a pseudo-intuition, you should try to build a relationship with your intuitive voice and come to know the manner of its communication. You may notice that intuitions are not accompanied by high states of emotion, excitement, and passion. Nor do they seek to rush you to action. Instead, intuition is received in a state of inner calmness and objectivity. This is because the source of intuition transcends ego. Pseudo-intuitions come from the ego and are therefore motivated by self-centered desires that are usually accompanied by emotions. Brunton says the three distinguishing marks of intuition are calmness, clarity, and certainty.

8) Reflect on any blocks that may hinder your receptivity to your intuition.

Everyone has the capacity of intuition. We are all connected to a higher source of intellect. However, we are all at different stages in our openness to this kind of communication. The wisdom of our intuitive mind is always present; it is the state of our own soul that determines our ability to receive its guidance and insight. If you reflect on your life, it is likely that you can recall times in your life when you have had some experience of intuition. On particular occasions you may find it difficult to reach this kind of intuitive guidance in your life. In such a circumstance, try to avoid accepting pseudo-intuition or the image of intuitive certainty, but instead rely on ordinary resources for solving your personal question. Continue your efforts in self-reflection and meditation and you will certainly cultivate a more intimate relationship with the wisdom of your higher self.*

How to Deal with Negative Voices

Even if one is able to develop one's ability to receive the guidance of intuition, what Brunton's thoughts make clear is that the greatest challenge is to discern this voice of wisdom from our beliefs, emotions, and prejudices. We may be able to receive the wisdom of the intuition, or daimon, but just as quickly we may reject it on account of some skepticism, doubt, or ignorance possessing us. In order to develop a clear dialogue with one's intuition, one must gain a clear understanding of the negative inner voices that arise in our lives.

One of the most effective ways to deal with negative voices within oneself is a very simple use of dialogue. The key to the study of the mental life is the transitions in our states of mind. If one becomes a good student of the inner life, the life of his or her own psyche, an interesting realization will occur. It is often the case that a very quiet and subtle thought, barely audible, has the power to change the course of our day. Often, though, these thoughts are not subtle at all but come crashing out as a thundering attack against us. In any case, whenever a negative thought or doubt arises, the approach to use is the same. Invite the voice to a dialogue, simply by asking the voice to express more fully and completely exactly what it is trying to say. You might notice that the voice within is startled at first. It doesn't expect an audience, and when it has one, it is often shy and rather inarticulate. It may wish just to repeat the charge. For example, you are trying to learn a musical instrument. The voice may say, "You can't do that." All of a sudden your state of mind toward this goal changes. Why is that? Then you realize, "Oh, it was this thought." At

---

*Paul Brunton, *The Wisdom of the Overself* (New York: E.P. Dutton, 1945), p. 373–380.

this point, ask the voice to explain itself: "Why can't I do that?" The voice may just restate the charge. But encourage it to answer completely. "You are not coordinated. You have no musical sensibility. You're too old." Do your best to get the voice to state its position, the charges it is laying out against you, as if it were a formal a

Once the charges are stated, you have the opportunity to consider whether they make sense. It is essential that you answer the charges. "I may not be coordinated now, but that is the whole point of taking music lessons and practicing." The voice may respond by saying, "But you'll never be great." And you answer, "How do you know? Even so, that is not my goal. My goal is to enjoy myself. And you never know if I'll be good at it until I practice." The voice goes on, "But you have no musical sensibility." You respond, "I have the sensibility to appreciate music and raise the desire to learn an instrument, so what are you talking about?"

What you will notice if you take on this practice is that the very activity of articulating the accusations will diminish their power. Moreover, once they are stated, you will see that they always contain some kind of faulty thinking. And when you answer them, this very activity will build an energy within you and restore your confidence and desire for your goal. If the voice is more stubborn, you may choose to discuss this inner dialogue with a friend. These are effective ways of dealing with these negative inner voices, but ultimately you may wish to discover why they arise in the first place. This demands serious reflection. Many turn to therapy to discover the root of these negative thoughts. In Appendix II, there is a brief introduction to a contemporary approach to self-reflection that uses the dialogic principles of Socrates.

7 ZEN AND THE ART OF DIALOGUE

In the Greek world, an art was a knowledge and power used for the benefit of one who was in need of the art. The archetypal example is that of the healer and the patient. The idea of art in the Zen tradition is very different. A Zen art, such as archery, swordsmanship, painting, or flower arrangement, does not aim to benefit another but is practiced for its own sake. The Zen art is a practice of transcending the ego. There can be no "other" to benefit, because the Zen master seeks to function free of such distinctions.

A most wonderful account of the training and practice of a traditional Zen art form is Eugene Herrigel's classic, *Zen and the Art of Archery*. The essence of the art is expressed in this marvelous passage from the introduction by the famous Zen scholar Daisetz T. Suzuki:

> In the case of archery, the hitter and the hit are no longer two opposing objects, but are one reality. The archer ceases to be conscious of himself as the one who is engaged in hitting the bull's-eye which confronts him. This state of unconsciousness is realized only when, completely empty and rid of the self, he becomes one with the perfection of his technical skill, though there is in it something of a quite different order which cannot be attained by any progressive study of the art. *

*Eugene Herrigel, *Zen and the Art of Archery* (New York: Vintage Press, 1971), p. vi.

Since the publication of *Zen and the Art of Archery* and the writings of people like Alan Watts, this idea has become part of Western culture. In the West, it is now generally recognized that one must let go of one's concept of self to enter fully into an activity. When one lets go of "self," one is unhindered by doubt and able to function unrestricted by any preconceived personal limitation. It is only when we are able to let go in this way that we are free to discover our highest potential.

In the Zen and Taoist traditions, when one allows one's actions to be guided by a greater power in such a way as to achieve an excellence that is effortless, it is called being one with the the *Way* or the *Tao*. In the Greek Pagan tradition, this is described as the power of the gods working through us. In the secular West, it is called just "being in the groove." No matter how it is described or what name it is given, the key to this kind of excellence lies in freedom from the limitations of one's conception of the self. Traditionally, this state has been cultivated through martial arts, flower design, calligraphy, and painting; in the contemporary world people are developing it in basketball (as documented by the Chicago Bulls' coach Phil Jackson in his book, *Sacred Hoops*), business, and many other activities.

Dialogue can also be pursued as an art that seeks this kind of excellence. In this respect, it is practiced both as good in itself and good for another, which according to Plato is the highest form of good. Yet, one may wonder, how can one transcend one's concept of self in a dialogue? This is an important question, especially since the primary teaching that is given to those practicing a Zen art is to avoid following one's thoughts and to let the mind reach a state of quietude that is free of thought. In a dialogue, however, one must cultivate a state of inner calm or coolheadedness *(sophrosyne)* as one allows the thought process to function. In approaching dialogue with the Zen spirit, one must stay focused on the issue at hand and not be distracted by thoughts that would lead one astray. As a listener, one needs to cultivate an emptiness and freedom from thought in order to remain open and receptive to what is being said. As a speaker, one seeks to speak appropriately and meaningfully to enhance the development of the dialogue without extraneous words.

In physical activities people are often able to let go of their thoughts of self and enter fully into their chosen art, as in the archery example. In the practice of Zen, one does not stop thoughts from arising—that is impossible, since the very nature of the mind is to think. The Zen student learns to avoid getting caught up in thoughts. Instead of following thoughts, the student learns to direct his or her attention to the space or interval between the thoughts.

When we get caught up in our thoughts, one thought leads to another so quickly that we don't even realize that we have become lost in the train of thoughts that has taken us on as passengers. In this state of mind we become passive and let the random and habitual patterns of our minds lead us. The problem is that they usually lead to a very undesirable way of being. We are taken along as we review somewhat arbitrary thoughts, often connected with concerns about the future or past, and our worries, angers, or fantasies. Frequently they lead us into very agitated and troubled states of mind.

And yet, even while traveling on this high-speed train, there is always an interval, perhaps the briefest of moments, but an interval nonetheless. Through training in Zen, or a similar discipline, one learns to focus on that interval and not to let the train go by, so to speak. With a little practice, one soon discovers that the interval between the thoughts widens, bringing a state of peace and calm to one's mind, as well as clarity and energy. With this clarity, we are able to allow our native intelligence to function much more freely and can see things about our individual lives and our world much more directly and spontaneously. In the practice of a Zen art, one becomes unhindered and undisturbed by any distracting thoughts that might interfere with one's practice. The goal is to allow oneself to enter completely into that interval between thoughts so that it appears that one is in a complete state of emptiness in which one realizes a much richer and ideal way of being. It is called a state of emptiness because it possesses an absolute purity and none of the qualities with which we are familiar, but it is really the opposite of empty because it is pregnant as the source and condition for all excellence. It is out of this state of mind that the greatest wisdom, excellence, and works of beauty emerge.

With training and practice, people are generally able to reach some level of competency in achieving this goal. When one engages in a physical art form, such as archery or flower arrangement, it is relatively easy to ignore one's thoughts and to focus completely on the activity. Each of us in our own way has had moments in life that approach the kind of one-pointed state that the Zen master cultivates regularly. For example, we are all able to separate our ego sense from the functioning of our bodies fairly easily. Each moment throughout the day our bodies move and respond in a multitude of ways that are not directly ordered by our conscious will. Take the simple act of walking down the street. We don't have to will each step. Each part of our body enters into the natural flow of walking without the need for conscious direction. In fact, if our bodies didn't function in this way, we wouldn't be able to do two things at once. Our conscious minds can focus on only one activity at a time, but, nonetheless, we are able to perform multitudes of tasks simultaneously: driving, typing, and sports are all examples. There is a natural wonder in each movement of the body that emerges if we reflect on the connection between our will and our actions. In his book, *Cheng Hsin: The Principle of Effortless Power*, martial arts champion Peter Ralston gives one example of this wonder in an imaginary dialogue with a reader:

Lift your hand.
How did you lift it?
I just lifted it.
Who lifted?
I did.
Now let's lift the hand again. Okay, you say you used your mind to lift it; you had the idea and made it happen. But how did you make it happen? You can leave your hand there and "think" about lifting it all day, you can scream and yell, ordering it to rise, but it will not. Not unless something else occurs. Your mind is not directly responsible for the hand lifting. Experience it. What is responsible? *

---

*Peter Ralston, *Cheng Hsin: The Principles of Effortless Power* (Berkeley, California: North Atlantic Books, 1989), pp. 39–40.

We can all appreciate the marvelous mystery of physical motion and its connection to our conscious will. It is because we are able to separate or distance our view of self from the body that we are able to function in Zen-like states. But in Zen, this questioning goes a step further into the realm of the mind. The Zen master asks:

> Think a thought.
> Where did it come from?
> I don't know. I just thought it.
> How long did it take?
> No time. It comes instantaneously.
> What thinks?

Does it take effort to have a thought? Do we have to will a thought to come? Does it take a thought in order to have a thought? This, of course, doesn't make sense because it would lead to an infinite regression of thoughts: thoughts of having a thought of having a thought of having a thought. Instead, apparently, thoughts just arise. But why do they arise? Why do they come when they do? Why do we think the particular thoughts that we do? Why do we have one particular thought instead of another? Are we in control of our thoughts? If we did have control of our thoughts, how would we change the thoughts that we think? Certainly, there would be many thoughts that would be eliminated—all the negative, critical, and false and harmful ones that persistently dissipate our energy and concentration. But negative thoughts can never be eliminated altogether. Therefore, we must conclude that we don't have this kind of control.

All the same, many seek to sell this idea that we can change our thoughts through training. There is no doubt that with training people can bring what they consider to be more positive thoughts into their minds. But they cannot eliminate the undesirable ones, though they can struggle to suppress them. In truth, when we attempt to suppress the negative thoughts, we initiate a battle within our psyche between our self-image and another, the more desirable self-image against the less desirable one. Zen practice, however, aims to go beyond the image of self altogether. We do not take on the Zen practice to reject or deny the self, but to recognize that at the heart of our existence is a grander mystery that is greater than our conception, so that any view of self is going to limit what is boundless. In dialogue, as in archery and other activities, the freedom from a concept of self is the condition for the highest excellence. This kind of excellence exists when act effortlessly and spontaneously in order to do what is appropriate, with nothing extra added. In one sense, this is nothing special, yet in another, it is magnificent. The highest ideal of dialogue is to act from the same state of mind.

In one respect, as a native speaker of a language we all possess this excellence. We bring to every conversation a perfect comprehension of conversational English, and this ability demands no effort. Spontaneously and instantaneously we recognize the very complex sounds uttered from a speaker's mouth, hear them as distinct words, and receive these words in their units of meaning as phrases, completely unaware that a complex procedure is taking place in our minds in every moment of the conversation. Then, with the same remarkable genius, we express our thoughts in language—articulating them in complex patterns, weaving them together in such a way as to communicate our ideas and feelings with accuracy and perfect skill. And this skill that we possess is equal to the skill of any master in any field, whether it be music, the visual arts, or the martial arts. We carry a perfect understanding of thousands of words as well as their various meanings and subtleties of use. We know how to combine them into grammatical sentences with a concern for rules governing past, present, and future tenses and the different moods, and the person. Clearly, the great genius of the human mind that is revealed through language and is present in everyone is a vivid mark of the greater mystery and greater intelligence that we all share.

Without Zen training, people approach their activities with very different goals in mind. Ordinarily, we seek to demonstrate our skill and thereby to express a self-image. This is the way most people also approach conversation. Conversation is seen as an opportunity to be witty, to show what we know, to be empathetic or understanding. It is a way of expressing our opinions and beliefs, with articulating views that we believe reflect our self-image. We define ourselves often with respect to our opinions about politics or religion as well as about family or social issues. We also define ourselves by how we react to certain issues. We are able to feel good about ourselves and righteous if we are outraged by some political action, and we also can characterize ourselves as people who are able to be objective and not show emotions. How then can dialogue transcend self?

Dialogue can transcend ego and self in that its ultimate aim is to share in something that goes beyond the ego, the ideal of truth and the spirit of the logos. Dialogue transcends ego if one recognizes that dialogue is not merely the interaction of two separate speakers, but the participation of two people in the logos. Dialogue is therefore the offspring of two people and not the sole property of either. A particular dialogue gains a life of its own through the participation of both speakers. The very things each dialogist says are not brought to birth from the individual alone, but from the dialogue itself. One dialogist presents thoughts to another, and those thoughts generate a flow of questions and statements that return to the first dialogist and become the cause of other new questions and statements, continuing this recursive process. To the degree that we are able to let go of ourselves and express what is appropriate, we can act like the master jazz improviser responding to the rhythmic and melodic interchange taking place between him and his fellow musicians or the master of aikido who reacts appropriately to an attacker with no more and no less force than is required.

Of course the thoughts expressed in dialogue are still *our* thoughts, as it were, but we take on a new kind of relationship to them. The aim of dialogue is to share an exploration of an issue, question, or idea. In the first place, this goal limits the thoughts that are considered appropriate to express. Second, we are functioning within a structure. If we are the answerer, we are expressing our view. We are not holding to that view or defending it like a possession, but bringing it to birth for evaluation as a subject for reflection. Moreover, in this activity we are following the guidance of our questioner and letting our minds respond unhindered to the inquiries because we seek to discover what opinions and beliefs are stored up in our minds. In one sense, it is very foolish to maintain a self-image that is connected to one's thoughts and beliefs. Our thoughts and beliefs continually come and go. As we age and gain greater experience and insight into life, our thoughts change and mature in depth, meaning, and significance. To cling to one's thoughts and opinions is literally to cling to the past and to limit one's growth.

If we are the questioner, on the other hand, our goal is to follow what is said without adding or taking away anything and to ask what is appropriate to make the question or issue clear. In this sense, the questioner is much like a detective on the trail of a mystery. His or her goal is not to theorize, but rather to bring out all the information and to investigate what is not clear or what is puzzling through further questioning. It should be a simple and organic process, not something contrived and preplanned in any way. In this respect, the questioner, too, is guided in his thoughts by the flow of the logos of the dialogue.

The integrity of the logos is the essential concept in dialogue. In dialogue, two minds come together to communicate about ideas through reason. Whereas each person certainly has a unique experience and approach to life, we all share in this power of reasoning, and this is what makes dialogue possible. It is the water that we human fish swim in. If reason did not exist, we could not communicate and understand one another, and we would not be able to reach agreements.

By entering into dialogue in the way we have been describing—in going beyond ego, not attaching firmly to one's thoughts or beliefs, searching for the truth, being open and sincere, entering a state of not knowing and mystery, respecting the logos, and expressing concern and respect for our dialogic partners—we are able to recognize this greater power called reason that functions through each of us and guides dialogue. When we open ourselves fully to this power, we are able to enter into dialogue with the spirit of a Zen master, that is, with the spirit of a Socrates. For Socrates, as we read earlier in *Theaetetus* and *Meno*, approaches dialogue barren of any beliefs, fully present in the moment and open to what is being expressed. He lives in a state of wonder and mystery, and from that state a wisdom emerges that is born from his puzzlement and stings his dialogic partners with the accuracy of an arrow shot from Apollo's silver bow. But this ability is also nothing special. Every child enters the world with this vision to see and question the obvious and thus reveal something that adults seek to hide.

The ultimate goal of this wisdom is to lead a friend to look at something in his life that is false and needs to be recognized if he is to grow. It is a deeply caring activity and one that ought to be approached with the greatest respect. Whenever it is taken on with even the slightest hint of ego, those who are questioned and challenged become wary, defensive, possibly even harmed, and will consequently become less willing to open themselves up to such a relationship. This situation is something we should strive to avoid, but even if we do get trapped in these roles, this hurt can always be healed by openly admitting that we were caught in an "ego game," for that, too, is a natural part of dialogue and can be expected to arise at times.

When we are able to tap into the power of reason, the power of the logos, we are able to participate in a genuine wisdom that can be used to see directly into the truth of our own lives and the lives of those around us. This wisdom is providential and brings about great benefit. With this wisdom, we can reach the highest aim of art, to benefit humanity, for this is the purpose for which Prometheus has given us these gifts. Whereas the archer or martial artist uses her art to defend a city and looks to an ideal of preservation, the dialogist engages in dialogue to help reveal the false, and does so by looking toward Truth as the ideal.

8 LOVE RELATIONSHIPS AND FAMILY

Fate and Providence in Love Relationships

The most important dialogic partner we will have in our lives is a spouse or beloved. We have been discussing how through dialogue one has the opportunity to gain personal growth and insight. The greatest catalyst for this kind of growth is a relationship with a significant other. It is through an intimate relationship with another that we reveal ourselves and allow ourselves to be seen truly as we are, free of any mask or appearance we may take on in society. The universe is designed in a most interesting way. That which we most desire in our lives is a romantic relationship, and the very condition for this kind of relationship is sincere dialogue. Dialogue allows lovers to know each other most intimately.

Since love demands that lovers show themselves fully and sincerely to each other, each is able to see what is best and most beautiful in the other. It is this vision of beauty that draws lovers together. Lovers then become great students of each other, attentive to and aware of the particular qualities and ways of the beloved. In this study they learn what is most beautiful about them and also what is not ideal. Lovers discover the imperfections of the beloved's character, and this makes love a most vulnerable affair.

We cannot disclose what is best without revealing what is worst, because in love we are in an open state where *all* is revealed. In this state there is no censor to hide what is bad. When, on occasion, such a censor emerges, it is immediately spotted and recognized by the lover as a mask, or false appearance. Even though this covering up is often done to hide a flaw or a problem, it also conceals the truth, for even flaws and problems have a truth, because they show where we are in our lives and therefore to what we must direct our attention for further growth. People take on roles or put on masks when they become fearful of making known something about themselves, fearful of simply presenting themselves as they are. Yet this is precisely what lovers desire to see. Thus, the best love relationship is one in which lovers unmask themselves and value this disclosure for showing what is best as well as whatever problems or difficulties exist. When lovers open up in this way, they are able to bring these problems into the relationship and can discover their beauty. For there is a magnificent beauty that exists in every sincere soul who has the courage to be honest with himself and the desire to become a more excellent human being.

The revealing of difficulties is a genuine baring of our humanity. Our mortal nature is defined by its very limitedness, and it has a continual concern and need for growth. This limitation is also the condition that creates a vast capacity for learning. As mentioned earlier, Socrates reported that he was always seeking his not knowing, that is, his limits; in the same way, we ought always to be open to our personal limitations. This is the difference between humans and gods in Greek mythology. Gods are perfect and have no limitations; therefore they are not in need of growth. Humans are imperfect and limited and in need of growth. According to the Greeks, to confuse oneself with a god is the greatest pitfall for a mortal, and it is given the name *hubris*. In the state of hubris, one loses his proper perspective of mortal nature and thereby loses touch with the purpose of human life. An individual is no longer in a position to recognize his inabilities and flaws and will not seek to grow. If he does not seek growth, he reaches a place of stagnation in his life or becomes caught in the fantasy that growth is unnecessary. Either way, he is not truly alive and actively engaged in the challenge of life. The drama of human growth is the very place where life gains its true meaning; if we are stagnating, we miss out on the great opportunities for growth that life is constantly presenting us. At the same time, we also invite tragedy into our lives, since the very function of tragedy is to awaken humans to our limitations.

Love relationships constantly show us our limitations, and for this reason relationships are perhaps the greatest human challenge. Love often fools us into the belief that relationships are the path to everlasting joy and the blissful life of the gods. And many of us are often terribly disappointed when we discover that this is not the case. When relationships become difficult, there is a great fall from this heavenly state, often accompanied by resentment, anger, and frustration. Many of us blame ourselves or our partners for this disillusionment, and this leads to tension. The heroic couples are those who are able to discover the secret of relationships—the fact that they are not easy. Those of us who can face the difficulties together and grow do so because we find a means of genuine communication.

Therein lies perhaps the greatest virtue of contemporary American society. Despite all the flaws and problems in our world, Americans have embarked on this greatest human challenge. Perhaps more than any other people in history, Americans are concerned with meaningful love relationships. With the rise of the woman's movement, the United States has made great strides in eradicating chauvinism from our society. This is not to say that there are not ongoing problems. For example, women are still paid much less than men for equal work. However, in many ways, women have the freedom to choose the kinds of lives they want to lead. Women now approach men as equals in society. They are in the position to speak their minds and challenge their husbands openly. They have the social and economic freedom to end their marriages if they find them unsatisfactory. And, consequently, this freedom presents men with a great challenge.

Women are generally more concerned with relationships and with intimacy, whereas men have a tendency to focus on their careers and personal goals (though, of course, there are always exceptions). In many cases, men are now, by necessity, being compelled to examine much more closely their lives and the ways they relate. They are being forced by their lovers to open up about themselves in ways they have never sought or desired to do. But, likewise, men are challenging women to open up and relate in ways that *women* are resistant to. With greater equality and responsibility, women must face the challenge of speaking their minds to men, which many women may find as equally fear-provoking as men find emotional vulnerability.

These blocks to more open communication can be the greatest hindrance to relationships. The very act of holding in our true feelings and thoughts about a situation or a relationship immediately creates a false appearance. Behind that false appearance begin the rumblings of our inner world and a personal drama unfolds that takes us away from the reality of our lives. No longer do we see clearly, but instead view the world through the projection of this inner drama. What is most dangerous is that we are often not aware of this projection. We are unable to see that the experiences of the present are colored and distorted by the active workings of these inner thoughts. They come before the mind and block our vision. To the degree that we are caught in certain beliefs about what is taking place in the present, beliefs created from past experiences and through which interpret life, do not truly live in the present, but instead live out a mixed life of experience and delusion.

An Example of a Drama in a Love Relationship

Imagine a husband and wife sitting on the couch reading. The wife is very open and loving to her husband. The husband feels as though his wife is demanding his attention. He does not wish at this moment to relate romantically. Yet he does not express this feeling because he thinks he may hurt his wife's feelings. Since he holds back his true thoughts, his wife begins to simply caress him. At this point, he feels that his space is being invaded and begins to tense. Then he withdraws from his wife and says he wants to read. His wife feels rejected and dissatisfied and replies that she does not feel loved. The husband, in turn, believes he is being criticized and becomes angry. The couple withdraw from each other, and both remain upset.

We all play out this sort of drama in our relationships. If you are able to recognize the drama in your relationship, write it out in as much detail as possible. The second step is to chart the stages and/or events through which the drama passes.

1. Reading on the couch
2. Wife is loving to husband
3. Husband wants to read but does not express this feeling
4. Wife caresses husband
5. Husband withdraws
6. Wife feels rejected
7. Wife says she does not feel loved
8. Husband gets angry
9. The couple withdraw from each other

In the next step we add states of mind to the stages:

1. Reading on the couch (husband and wife are relaxed)
2. Wife is loving to husband (wife is open and loving)
3. Husband wants to read but does not express this feeling (husband is concerned and does not want to hurt wife's feelings)
4. Wife caresses husband (wife still loving, husband tense)
5. Husband withdraws
6. Wife feels rejected (wife feels hurt)
7. Wife says she does not feel loved (wife feels dissatisfied)
8. Husband gets angry (feels as though he is being criticized and put down)
9. The couple withdraw from each other (both are upset)

Once the drama is charted out in this way we must examine it. It is necessary to pay attention to both the positive states of mind and the negative ones—and the transitions between the two. In the drama outlined here we start out with a very positive state of mind. However, it soon makes the transition to a negative state, partly because the husband does not express what he feels. He wants to avoid hurting his wife's feelings, but in the end he does so anyway.

At the point when the wife makes certain advances to reveal her state of mind to her husband, he has the opportunity to express his own desires and state of mind. (We should be careful when we hide our true thoughts and be attentive to the consequences, because it very often leads to an undesired outcome.) However, if he says that he does not want to relate affectionately at this time, he may still hurt his wife's feelings. It is important to consider whether the wife is interested in making love or in simply being together affectionately on the couch as they each continue to read. It is also to important to consider whether it is a pattern in the relationship that the husband is not interested in these options. Why is the husband not interested in making love? Or in the example given, why does the husband feel as though his space is being invaded when his wife is simply caressing him?

On the other hand, the wife must also consider why she feels rejected. If there is a repeated pattern, it is a much better idea to raise it for discussion and dialogue. It is often more difficult to discuss an important issue in a relationship when it arises as the consequence of a drama. In our scenario, the wife starts complaining to her husband, and this "pushes his buttons" and sets him off. Why does the wife choose these opportunities to bring up her concerns about the relationship rather than other times, when the husband may be more objectively prepared to consider them?

It is likely that she does so because it fullfils the needs of the drama. Once the husband becomes angry, the wife can hold on to her feeling of rejection and her belief that the relationship will not improve and can in this way prolong the state of dissatisfaction. The husband, in turn, gets angry and achieves a separation from his wife in the house, thus avoiding dealing with the question of intimacy. Instead he can play out the role of being independent.

It takes a great deal of self-reflection, honesty, and diligence to arrive at this kind of objective view of one's relationship and one's life. Once this dynamic is revealed and the roles are identified, the next step is to consider why we play out such a role and what it blocks us from achieving in our relationships. In this particular example, the husband needs to contemplate why he cuts off his wife's expression of love, and the wife must think about why she does not express her concerns more directly, and also why she holds on to feelings of dissatisfaction.

If the husband and wife reflect on these questions, they will discover that the structure and drama of their own relationship is shaped and molded by their experience as children in their own families, watching the model their own parents provided for love relationships. Upon reflection, the husband discovers that he interprets his wife's affection as an image of his mother's desire for his attention. Moreover, in his relationship with his mother he did not feel free to express his own needs, but feared that his mother would feel rejected. And he sees that there was a fear of intimacy in his family, which he now shares. There was also the belief in his home that it was important not to feel dependent upon one's beloved, and so he sees value in his independence.

The wife, on the other hand, sees that her father and older brother were often cold to her, which made her feel rejected. Now she sees an image of them in the actions of her own husband. Furthermore, she was taught by her mother that this is just the way men are—cold and aloof—but that women are the opposite—warm and loving. This attitude provided the justification for her mother's inevitable dissatisfaction, which she expressed in the home. And so the wife discovers that she is playing out the role of her mother and adopting the same state of mind in her own home. Since she was taught that men would never change, she has concluded that there is no use in raising this issue for serious discussion.

In this example, the husband and wife are no longer dealing with what is happening in the present, but are seeing present actions within an interpretive framework of the past. And once this happens, states of mind arise that have the power to initiate drama.

Because the husband is tense, he withdraws, and because the husband withdraws, the wife feels rejected. These interactions undoubtedly lead the couple to retreat into their own minds and their own reflections. This turning inward and away from the truth and experience of the present further contributes to the power of the false inner drama at work, which consequently leads to greater tension in the relationship as both people begin to perceive the other not as they are, but through the projected images of their respective parents or other family members. The tension of these inner dramas is projected outward and forms the basis for new external dramas until they reach their climax and must be resolved in some way. As we discussed earlier, no state of mind can last indefinitely. The tension will be resolved, and the couple will begin the cycle again, or they will gain insight into the reasons for the problems manifested in the relationship.

This is the working of Fate. It plays itself out in ways that are similar to the cause and effect relationships of the natural world. Just as things in nature are predisposed to behave according to regular patterns, so, too, are we limited to the patterns we learned as children. Just as the tides ebb and flow according to the cycles of the moon, similarly, individuals within a relationship follow certain patterns of behavior and enter into a series of states of mind that constitute the dramas of their particular lives. The difference is that as humans we are conscious and have the opportunity to become aware of these patterns and to live with a greater degree of mindfulness. We must certainly pass through cycles and dramas, but the challenge is to learn from them, to gain insight and grow, striving for higher and better ways of being, continually pursuing a richer and fuller life, limitless in its potential for beauty and excellence.

To attempt to deal with the difficulties that arise from these problems, many Americans have turned to counseling. In one way our concerns derive from the fact that we are the most neurotic and unhealthy people that have ever existed. As many thinkers have pointed out, Americans have destroyed most of the institutions and values that maintain a healthy society, namely, close-knit families, a sense of community, a slow-paced lifestyle, walking, eating fresh food, maintaining ritual as a part of life, and so on. Instead, we live alone, separated from families, moving from place to place, changing jobs, driving in our cars alone at seventy miles an hour, watching TV—stressed-out from the pace of technology, the demands of work, and limited vacation time. Our way of life itself causes personal crises.

When such crises occurs, we seek out the deeper reasons for personal problems. According to the Greek Wisdom tradition, such problems are a form of illness passed down through the false beliefs of a family. Although these problems were thought to have been present in families for countless generations, there was no particular urgency to investigate them, since they united the family in its functioning in a stable society. In our unstable and highly competitive society, however, there is no benefit to holding on to such problems and false beliefs, and so we have the opportunity to gain a greater insight into our lives and relationships. We revere individuality and have the social and economic freedom to free ourselves from the traditional bonds of family connections. We are prepared to challenge the family and religious traditions that shaped us. Our goals, therefore, are to have healthier and more ideal relationships and family lives than previous generations— perhaps than any other previous generation. In the midst of our insane society, the dilemmas of our inner lives have been revealed; perhaps by looking at this inner world more closely and seeking out genuine growth in this realm, we will be able to become better people and reshape our society and our world to fit a higher vision of life.

Our love relationships are essential to this process but, of course, they present the greatest challenges. Love is the greatest bond of Fate; it is what ties us to our families. Yet we leave our parents to start our own families, and it is this same bond that directs us. Somehow, in the most wondrous and amazing way, we discover other individuals with whom we can maintain the bonds of love. And when we do, we find that this bond that has made us so happy also brings with it all the difficulties and problems that we experienced in our relationships with our parents and siblings. It is certainly a manifestation of the yin and yang principle that love and problems, the highs and lows, the joys and difficulties are intertwined such that one cannot exist without the other and each implicitly contains the other. When we find our beloved, we also find a psyche who shares many, if not all, the ways of being of our parents, and therefore a person with whom we are able to play out some form of the family drama we have inherited.

Is It Just Opposites That Attract?

Common wisdom states that opposites attract each other. This is obviously true to a degree, but there is another aspect to this picture of relationships. In a beloved we find someone who appears to be our opposite and foil, but who at the same time, with close observation and learning, we discover is remarkably like ourselves. And because of this profound likeness, our beloved displays the qualities we most love about ourselves, as well as those we most dislike. We see in our beloved our own limitations; often none of this is readily apparent, but is instead slow to emerge and reveal itself. Consequently, most of the fights and disagreements between lovers are really a consequence of our own inner division. We lash out at our own limitations and problems, the things we don't like about ourselves. And we place the blame on the shoulders of our beloved, who to some extent has these problems. But in another sense, it is pure projection. Think about it—why else would the things our lovers do bother us so much? If we were happy with ourselves and our own characters, would we really be disturbed by seeing these problems in another? Probably not. Instead, we would have compassion for the other. But when we are incensed and filled with anger and frustration, it is really because what we see in another are our own limitations manifest for our view.

Let me provide an example of how this takes place in a relationship. A man falls in love with a woman who is very quiet and keeps her thoughts to herself. They get married, and when she does speak up it concerns her desire for everything in the relationship to be perfect and the dissatisfaction she feels when it is not. In this respect, she is very critical of the husband. The husband, on the other hand, at first does not think they are alike in these respects at all. He is very verbal and enjoys speaking his mind. He considers himself rather easygoing and not a perfectionist by any stretch of the imagination. Moreover, he thinks himself to be the kind of person who is accepting of other people's limitations and is very understanding. Here we have an example of a couple who appear to display very different qualities and who consider themselves, especially in these ways, the very opposite of each other. But as their relationship matures and the two people gain a deeper understanding of themselves and each other, they come to see their relationship more accurately.

Whereas the wife is very quiet and faces the challenge of speaking her mind, the husband soon discovers that although he is willing to speak up in most situations, in very significant situations, where he is challenged to speak his mind to an authority figure, he closes up in the very same way as his wife. And although he may be easygoing about most things, he also has very high standards and is a perfectionist when it comes to those matters that are most important to him. Whereas he is understanding and accepting of other people's limitations, there are exceptions. With the people who are most important in his life he is not this way at all, but holds them to high critical standards. In fact, he discovers that he has the same critical and demanding attitude that his wife has toward him. The wife, on the other hand, in the course of reflecting on her life, discovers within herself a remarkable power for speaking out (very much like her husband's) but a power which she had been restraining.

This idea that our own dissatisfaction and difficulties with our loved ones are the consequence of what we see in ourselves is a profound one. It suggests that there is a true justice ordering our lives. The power of Fate that draws us to our lovers and binds us in those relationships with all their joy and difficulty creates a situation in which in our love for another we must constantly be facing ourselves. This suggests that the very aim of relationships is not merely happiness or contentment, but the higher goal of "knowing thyself." And it shows that this challenge is not a solitary one, but takes place in the union of a most beautiful and intimate relationship with one's beloved. The problems that we discover in our fated existence lead to the higher good found in personal growth. For this reason, the sages of the ancient world concluded that Fate itself is governed and directed by the higher principle of goodness called Providence.

Principles of Dialogue in Love Relationships

In love relationships, more than in any other, we are vulnerable to the power of our emotions. In such a relationship we must approach dialogue in a much different way than we do in our other relationships. In love we are very often up to our noses in the sea of emotions that binds us. Our love relationships affect our entire being. It is, therefore, foolish to suppose we can enter into these dialogues with complete objectivity, logically, and with a clear head. If we believe this, we are fooling ourselves. At the same time, though, we do not have to abandon the reasonable approach to dialogue that we have been outlining. The principles and the ideal of dialogue remain. But lovers need to recognize that there is a greater need in romantic relationships than is in other contexts to allow for flexibility when using the model of dialogue.

Lovers ought to try to focus on a specific question or issue. Yet, any question in such a relationship is going to bring up many other questions and issues as well, because romantic relationships are so much more complicated than other relationships. Lovers ought to acknowledge that it is important to voice those other issues at times, though they should try to return to the main issue. Lovers also demand much more patience from each other. It is essential that they allow a great deal of time for dialogue. Significant issues are often very difficult to clarify and resolve; therefore, these dialogues demand a relaxed pace—that is, no deadlines. If for some reason lovers are restricted to a certain amount of time, they can agree that they don't have to finish the dialogue at one sitting but are willing to return to it the next day or whenever possible.

In love relationships we often are trying to persuade another to agree with what we think is right or how we want the other to act. And quite often lovers return to the same themes over and over and over again with very little progress. We try to persuade our lovers to be more open, more aggressive in their business lives, more tidy, more loving, more understanding, less interested in sports and friends, more interested in love, or to give up drink, cigarettes, gambling, or drugs. In these kinds of dialogues the same pattern repeats itself. It is as if we are playing out a drama on the stage, each person with a role and well-rehearsed lines. As one lover speaks, the other prepares his or her well-known response, then becomes filled with the need to express these thoughts, and can hardly hold back, even when he or she knows it will do no good. (These thoughts may even be the very words that make our partners angry and enraged.)

The back-and-forth responses are like moves in a well-rehearsed dueling match. Each thrust is met with a parry, and the intensity grows and grows, pushing further and further to a number of possible climaxes—a painful and frustrating stalemate, a desire to just end the relationship, anger, rage, or even violence. And as in any drama, each climax is followed by a denouement, or resolution. This is a necessity, because no human being can remain in the intense state of that climax, whatever form it takes, for very long. The climax must be resolved. Often it is resolved through a temporary truce, with or without understanding. It may lead to temporary separation (either emotional or physical). Many lovers go through this cycle of fighting, followed by a release of tension and a return to intimacy and passion. The resolution then brings one back to the relationship in a fresh way, and the lovers begin anew like the cycle of the seasons—from a kind of wintry death the relationship returns to the spring of life, and the drama begins once again.

There is always going to be a cycle and drama in our relationships and in our lives. There is no way to avoid it, because it is the very nature of life. What we need to do is learn from these cycles so that the same ones don't continue to repeat themselves. Instead, we need to create a spiral in which our lives and relationships evolve, and with each cycle we gain deeper insight and understanding of ourselves and one another and allow the drama to spiral upward like the leaves of a plant growing up its stalk, yielding a richer and more bountiful fruit. This is not easy. In order to accomplish such growth, we must first recognize that there is such a repeating pattern in our relationship. We can do this by charting out the states of mind and the events of the particular drama and watching it unfold. Ideally, we should do this with our lover, but if necessary, it can be done alone and then shared with our partner as an object of dialogue.

Once we chart out the drama of our relationships, we will see certain patterns emerge. We will also become more aware of the moments when our partners appear to be "pushing our buttons," as people often say. It is precisely at these times that we may feel compelled to respond. In this response it is likely that we desire to express certain concerns that we would most like our partners to understand and accept. These are the words that often seem most important to us, and the most vital to fairness, and they represent what we most desire in our relationships and in our lives. In the best of situations, our partners will understand and accept them. We are considering those things that seem most obvious and natural to us, but which our partner doesn't seem to grasp. Instead, when we express them, our lovers seem resistant, which causes frustration and adds to the emotional intensity of the discussion.

If we recognize that these thoughts do not advance the discussion, it is essential to try a different approach. It is at this particular moment in the dialogue that we must put our thoughts aside temporarily and look at the situation differently. When our partner pushes our buttons and we feel compelled to express these thoughts that are usually not helpful, stop at that moment and try to pay special attention to exactly what our partner is saying and what his state of mind is. Instead of bringing up their concerns in response to our partner, open up to his concerns. It is precisely at this moment that there is a potential for a significant breakthrough in the relationship, if we consider that our lover may be saying something that we genuinely need to reflect upon. There is always going to be a degree of truth in what our partner is saying, and we need to accept that and see how it presents new possibilities in the dialogue and a new way of looking at the issue.

If in that moment we don't get angry, but instead open up, our partner will gain the opportunity to relax the powerful forces driving her to push our buttons, and she might see the issue more clearly. If we let ourselves receive what she is saying and give it sincere consideration, it may give our partner the chance to change her view of the entire relationship, because she is probably thinking (just as we are), "He is never going to get it; he is never going to change." If we listen to what she is saying, it will release her from her locked-in and limited vision of us, which allows the spiraling upward to begin. This is very difficult, because it demands that we take in something that we may reject, hate, or fear. But it is essential to recognize that we *may* be deluded in some way about what we reject, hate, or fear. And this is the very thing that is the key to the growth of the relationship.

Most often in a love relationship, conversations about problems become a free-for-all, where each party presents his concerns and the other either defends herself or directs the conversation toward another related issue or aspect of the relationship. These discussions very often function as a means merely to voice all the little annoyances and some of the big problems that we hold inside in the course of daily life with our loved ones. In any relationship there is usually a lot that concerns us, so much that it would be very difficult to constantly bring up these issues. These discussions are very healthy ways to relieve the tension that results from holding our thoughts back, but usually understanding and insight cannot be gained in the midst of them, but must come after all the negative thoughts are vented. This venting brings relief and clarity to the discussion, at which point people can finally come to an understanding. Although some of the thoughts that are expressed may be very significant, it is a good idea to clear out everything that has been held in before a couple begins the serious and focused work of a real dialogue such as we have been outlining. Simply put, the two individuals must be in the proper state of mind to commit to a dialogue, which may require that they air some of their grievances first. Then an important transition can be made toward focusing on what is the essential or most important issue or question that needs to be considered by the couple, which in turn can become the subject of the dialogue.

When the dialogue begins, the lovers can take appropriate roles. If there is something of concern to one individual in the relationship, he can raise the point. The other should do her best to listen and consider all the points being made. What is important and most difficult is not to immediately reject what is being said and rush to defend oneself, but instead to listen and look at the full picture. This is what your lover is seeing and thinking in this moment; this is what they desire to deal with. It is helpful to consider Socrates' principle that what one thinks to be true may or may not be so. What is being said may be true, and it may not. Do not consider it just as a charge that must be defended, but as a claim that can equally be true or false. In this way, we can attempt to be objective in the discussion. For it is likely that even if much of what is said is not true, there is some truth in what our lovers are seeing, which can provide an opportunity for us to gain an insight that can be immensely beneficial to ourselves and our relationships.

Is Love Rational?

When we ask whether love is rational, we must distinguish this question from another—that is, is love logical? *Logical* is the word that we use to talk about the mechanical functioning of computers and calculators according to fixed systems of rules. *Rational* is a much broader term. The idea of reason and rationality in the classical sense makes room for the passion and mystery of love. It is important to consider this question because it raises the issue of whether we can rationally determine what kind of love relationships we want to be in. When we ask this question, we attempt to put into words our ideal of a love relationship. This very act of putting into words our ideal is a rational and reasonable act. We might say we desire a man or woman who is kind and generous, for example. Another may seek one who is deeply honest, or passionate and romantic, or creative, or intelligent. Each of us has a vision of the kind of mate we seek in life. When we put into words the kinds of qualities we most desire in another and imagine such a lover, this ideal becomes an object of desire. When we think about it, this ideal fills us with passion and the longing to be with such a person.

But why? What is the nature of this attraction? Why are we drawn to one kind of individual as opposed to another? What is the nature of the desire and longing that we feel? What is the nature and power of the beauty that we see in this ideal? We all can agree that it is one of the most powerful forces in our lives, something that lifts us out of our ordinary way of being to an exalted state. This is the great mystery of love, and it can be appreciated and cultivated through words. By expressing our ideal most clearly, we paint a vivid picture and are able to gain an understanding of what it is that draws us in the realm of love. In this respect, love is rational.

Once we have expressed our ideal, it can be used as a standard for our relationships. In Plato's view, it is this very ideal that unites lovers. You may wish to experiment and discover whether you and your lover (or prospective lover) share a common ideal. Simply consider what quality you most desire in another. Try to capture it in one word or phrase. It is the quality that we find most attractive in the kinds of people with whom we desire to have a sustained and intimate relationship. In some respects there are many different qualities that we desire, but in this activity we try to articulate the primary quality that we find desirable. This quality can become an object for dialogue with one's lover. If two people are in love, it is likely that they share the same ideal, or one that is very similar. If it turns out that you and your lover don't, you might consider the effect that this difference has on your relationship. To the degree that we do share a common vision of life with another, we are able to commune with them and be one. To the degree that there is a significant difference, there is a lack of unity. If a lack of unity is perceived, it would be important to reflect on its impact in the relationship and how each individual feels about the relationship.

When lovers first confront problems, they must do so in many ways, alone and fearful about their future together. Although the conflicts within a relationship often pose these risks and cause great pains, those who meet this challenge will find out that even these struggles have been directed by a greater power. They will realize that the conflict itself has led the relationship to a higher plateau. And the more two lovers engage in this challenge, the greater the vision and strength they will have in their relationship and the higher the peaks they will travel to together. When lovers learn to put their vision of life and love into words, they discover something remarkable. Love depends on understanding, and understanding arises most vividly through words. When lovers are able to learn the art of dialogue, they gain the power to move away from a lack of understanding, and its accompanying discord, to the concord and unity of genuine understanding. In this movement couples develop penetrating insight into themselves and each other. They also learn that they can open up, be vulnerable, and face their difficulties and problems together. They gain the confidence to confront the pain and unease of such difficult encounters, and they find that there exists something much more real and significant that unites them and provides the power to transcend problems—understanding.

Lovers must also discover the great significance of expressing what is beautiful about our relationships. Dialogue does not exist to examine difficulties alone. It also is a means of exploring the beauty, wonder, and joy of love. Lovers possess a great source of power—a vision of the beauty of their beloved. It is essential to express this vision. When we do, it enters into our beloveds like a stream of beautiful and divine light, filling them with beauty, and this power, in turn, allows them to reveal themselves in their most beautiful light. This then has an even more powerful effect on the lover, who is filled with the beautiful sight. The beloved then may share his or her vision of the other in words, and so this power moves from one to the other and from the other to the one, each playing both roles and uniting in the bonds of the beauty that they see in each other.

Family

The natural consequence of a family relationship is sexual union and the birth of children. The raising of children and communication within the family offers a special challenge to dialogue as well. This is because young children do not have the capacity to articulate what they see and desire in the same way that adults do. And so adults must make a special effort to put themselves in the minds of their children.

In a dialogue, the dialogists see each other as friends and must enter into communication as equal partners. There is no authority role, which, of course, challenges the traditional parent-child relationship. When parents enter into dialogue with their children, they must temporarily put aside their roles as authorities and knowers. They must open themselves up to their children as concerned friends in a very important relationship. This attitude gives children the opportunity to express their own vision of the world. It also introduces them to the principles of friendship and trust. In this way parents provide their children with an environment that nurtures their children's intellect and wisdom. Yet this environment is the greatest danger for parents, because in it children have the ability to challenge their parents about what they see around them and about their activities. In this way, children function just as a lover does, but in a more powerful way, because children come into this world with no prejudices or preconceptions. They are like Zen masters in their ability to see things just as they are. And whereas children have this all-seeing capacity, parents have the omnipotent power to silence them, which is what usually happens. Consequently, children learn to blind their own capacity for seeing the world clearly and mute their power of expressing it.

But there is another way. According to Grimes, all events in a family that have a potential for limiting a child's growth can be reconciled if parents attend to one simple act. We as parents merely have to provide our child with an open environment in which the child is free to speak clearly and honestly about what he sees without any fear of punishment or other negative consequences. Parents don't necessarily have to agree with what children say. We simply have to treat our children as we would any other friend—expressing what we think and being open to considering what the child says. We must make clear that we value what the child has said and will think it over carefully. In the end, we as parents must act according to what we think is best, and we ought to say so; at the same time,

9 DIALOGUE IN THE WORKPLACE

The Ideal of Dialogue in the Workplace

The workplace offers us a unique context in which to practice dialogue as a means to better communication. Unlike relationships within the family, in the workplace we are expected to relate to one another in an objective and rational way. Work situations usually concern trying to get something accomplished, and they therefore lend themselves to this rational approach. Consequently, many discussions in the workplace follow the principles of a good dialogue naturally, without the conscious recognition of a formal structure. There exists a focused question or topic, and participants seek the truth of the issue. They approach it as friends and not competitors, and they follow each other's words.

There are many benefits to this model for work situations. For one, things get done. Because this is a rational model that leaves aside personalities and emotions, individuals are able to stick to the issue at hand. The first principle of the model is to stay focused on the particular question. When this is done, people are productive—they move toward practical and creative solutions to problems.

Secondly, people are genuinely empowered. This means they are free to use their minds and to actively explore the issue at hand. In these situations they are in a position of responsibility to make things better, which makes one's particular job, and therefore one's life, meaningful. Human beings are naturally seekers of truth. We like puzzles and mysteries, and these kinds of activities gain in value when they contribute to a productive end.

The valuable goals of the workplace are many. They can be the challenge of a CEO working with advisers and board members to find the appropriate direction for their company, computer programmers working together to find a solution in their program design, teachers working together to improve the curriculum for their school, or doctors and nurses discussing the best procedures for an emergency room. In all these situations, people feel most valued and alive when they are participating in some way in addressing the particular problems of their jobs.

This is, of course, the ideal. In actuality there are just as many reasons why people avoid these kinds of dialogues at work. When we enter into such dialogues, we do not always do so in an ideal manner, but instead as human beings with our individual peculiarities and differences of personality and temperament. In a dialogue in the workplace, there is always the possibility that we may encounter individuals with serious personal problems that manifest themselves in these situations and are then projected on to others. Employees must face bosses and whatever problems the boss may have (whether minor personality conflicts or the deeper issues of sexism or prejudice). Bosses must deal with their employees and the possibility that an employee is projecting personal problems into the workplace. Coworkers must relate with one another and address a multitude of problems that may arise.

Work, perhaps more than any other life situation, is the arena of the ego. In the United States individuals often identify with their occupations. Whether we work in a steel plant, as an engineer, or as a business manager, our jobs often comes with a certain image—what we call the ego—and with ego comes the desire for success and praise, as well as the fear of failure and blame.

The ego is characterized by a movement between these two

extremes of praise and blame, and each person follows a different kind of motion. Some sway from extreme to extreme very quickly, as if suspended like a heavy pendulum from a tall crane; others stay relatively balanced, touching these poles on more rare occasions. The life of an individual and the particular motion of the psyche and the patterns it follows are governed by the power of Fate. People follow different patterns of life, just as plants do. There are those plants that are fast-growing and short-lived and others that are slow-growing and long-lived; there are those that die each season and others that live through the winter. Each plant needs a special kind of care and, in a similar way, there are many different kinds of management styles employed by ingenious experts in business and psychology to deal with diverse people and their manifold particularities.

The dialogic approach, on the other hand, presents a much more simple ideal. It is the ideal of friendship. The word *friendship* is not meant to express the ordinary concept of friendship, which implies an informal means of relating. In the ideal that we are discussing, the principle of friendship can be followed in a very formal setting. By friendship we mean a state of unity, as opposed to a state of enmity, the latter which is characterized by conflict and rivalry. The ideal of friendship is one that can be cultivated between individuals and also within ourselves. Such a state of unity is considered the condition for doing anything well. In a state of unity, we are not distracted by internal or external conflict but remain focused and concentrated. We are able to become absorbed in what we are doing and achieve a condition in which we are no longer conscious of the flow of time. We all fall into this kind of state of mind in some activities in our lives, whether it is work, sports, or making love; most of us would describe the times when we are in this state of mind as the peak experiences of our lives. When we achieve a state of unity and friendship with ourselves, we are in a much better position to share in this ideal within a group. When a group functions according to the ideal of friendship, it is unified in pursuit of a common goal (or goals) and is willing to put aside particular differences for the sake of the goal. The group members share the common desire to discover what is both true and best in terms of each issue that arises along the path that leads toward the goal. There is a freedom to discuss and consider together whatever difficulties arise in this pursuit, that is, a spirit of complete openness and honesty that encourages people to voice their concerns, questions, and thoughts without fear of retribution. In their work, group members share a commitment to the model of dialogue, and consequently trust that their thoughts will be given a fair hearing by co-workers and managers and can become the subject of an open dialogue.

In a workplace guided by the ideal of friendship, there will be no rivalry and competition. So, for example, workers will always be willing to share information and knowledge. In an unfriendly work situation, on the other hand, workers strive to get ahead of one another and therefore hold back their knowledge and assistance in order to see their colleagues fail. This kind of work relationship is very harmful to individual lives, to particular businesses, and to society. It fosters a spirit of division and conflict within and between people. And such a rivalrous spirit not only exists in the business world but is present even in the work environments of teachers, doctors, and public servants.

The principle of friendship, according to the ancient Greeks, is the most important principle in any combined effort amongst people. It is through this kind of friendship that people are united, and this unity is the essential condition for the achievement of any goal. The opposite of unity is strife and conflict, and in such circumstances it is very difficult, and often impossible, to achieve any kind of good. It was through unified effort that the ancient Greeks were able to defeat a Persian army that outnumbered tenfold. The Greeks fought in a form called the phalanx. They stood together shield to shield, and as long as this unified front was maintained, their enemy faced a literal wall of resistance. It was because of their commitment to an ideal of friendship and unity that they were able to work together so effectively.

Applied in the business world, this model leads to a situation in which workers and employees can trust a "win-win" principle.

According to Zen teacher and businessman Gerry Wick, "If you support the people who work for you, they will push you up. If you support your superiors, they will pull you up."* We can add that if you support your coworkers, everyone will benefit in the creation of a better work environment, a more productive business, and greater opportunity. (Opportunity is often limited in a particular workplace, but when good work is achieved, it will bring about opportunities for advancement both inside and outside a particular business.)

This ideal, however, challenges many of the traditional ways in which business has been conducted in the United States. In large corporations, a hierarchical system of management was developed in which, quite often, managers have complete power over their subordinates. This world is defined by the so-called corporate ladder—individuals contend against one another and, according to the metaphor, are required to step upon one another to get ahead and move upward.

There are still many work milieus that follow this model of management, whether the companies are large or small, public or private. It is essential for workers to look at their situations and consider the reality of their work environment. We ought not live under the delusion that we are in a friendly environment when we are not. Conversely, we should not consider that we are in an unfriendly environment when it is in fact a friendly one. In both instances, a false view of our workplace can lead to conflict and the possible loss of our position.

If we find ourselves in an unfriendly place, we at least have the option of talking openly with our employer and coworkers and getting them to put into words the modus operandi of the workplace. If we don't work within an ideal context, the second best option is to find a place where people can be honest about the nature of the situation. In this way, workers can play according to the requirements of the particular game, with no need for inner

---

*Gerry Shishin Wick Sensei, "Zen in the Workplace: Approaches to Mindful Management," *Tricycle: The Buddhist Review*, 5, No. 4 (1996), pp.14–19.

conflict or conflict with coworkers. It is also possible that encouraging coworkers to articulate what is really taking place may allow them to see that they are unhappy with the status quo. A dialogue may lead to the consideration of other possibilities and thus to the improvement of the work environment.

Amidst all the changes in the contemporary workplace, this top-down management style is losing its hold over the business world. In the past ten years or so, as companies have drastically reduced and eliminated middle management, a new work environment has been created. The new workplace is becoming dominated by an increasingly complex technology and a need for more intercommunication between coworkers who rely on one another rather than compete against one another. And these diverse workers are being led by team managers whose job is to empower employees and improve communication, not tyrannize them. Although this leveling out of the hierarchy has eliminated many jobs, one of its great benefits is that it has in many ways liberated the workplace from the abundance of managers and bosses that hindered open dialogue. The new workplace has a structure that is dependent upon the exercise of effective dialogue among workers. Therefore, those who are educated in this skill have an important asset and will be able to make a meaningful contribution to their workplace.

Principles for Dialogue in the Workplace

In order to bring the principles of dialogue into our work relationships, we have to create the foundation for dialogue. Dialogue is a commitment that people enter into willingly. In relationships and friendships, there is usually an implicit commitment to the spirit of dialogue. In the workplace such a commitment does not necessarily exist. Often coworkers will not be interested in dialogue, especially if it cuts into personal time. In order to create a context for dialogue, it may be necessary to educate our fellow workers concerning the principles and benefits of dialogue.

In a dialogue there are no bosses. Just as parents must temporarily put aside their role as authorities in order to engage in a dialogue, so also must bosses and managers. A dialogue is a time when we put aside our roles and speak openly and honestly. The goal is to get the information out clearly and evaluate it together. A similar situation exists in the military and is often portrayed on *Star Trek: The Next Generation* in cases where a subordinate officer asks his commander if he may speak candidly. When the subordinate officer makes this request, he is asking that the ordinary relationship be suspended temporarily to make room for a special kind of communication free of military protocol. Similarly, a dialogue in the workplace is ideally an opportunity for employees and bosses to put aside their roles and evaluate the issue independently of authority, praise, or blame.

We must recognize that this attempt is always accompanied by risk. We never know how the other person will react. This is true not only with authority figures in the workplace but in all our relationships. When we are honest, there is always a risk. Just because a boss or manager has agreed to a dialogue does not mean that he or she will not react negatively. This is the reality of life. However, we must take such a risk to achieve a better working relationship. If it doesn't work out, we may still benefit from discovering that the relationship and position were inevitably leading to conflict, and we can take the opportunity to find a new job. With an appreciation for dialogue, we can also seek out a new position and working relationships with people who are more open to this form of communication.

Although the workplace is supposed to be an objective context, the reality is very often the complete opposite. Humans cannot avoid bringing their individual dramas and the workings of their particular fates into any situation. All too often, people expect others to act in a professional and objective manner and are slow to respond when someone is not doing so. To suppose that personal issues are not going to arise is naive—we must expect them and be on the lookout for them. Ideally, we can build working relationships in which our fellow workers will be able to acknowledge this fact and therefore be willing to recognize when their own problems emerge. If this is the case, we are quite fortunate because we can trust that a coworker will be willing to deal with these issues. If not, it may be necessary for us to wait for the cycle to play itself out before we can communicate with our coworkers again.

At the same time, let us not forget the issue of projection and our own roles in the workplace drama. To the degree that we become caught up in the problems of other people, we are moved by our own fate and we need to reflect on this. A group of workers is very much like a family. We are accepted into the work environment and chosen by its leaders, very often for the same reasons that we are chosen by our lovers. We may be the kind of person who can take on the appropriate role in the drama of the workplace. We may be the kind of person who is willing to accept the brunt of the boss's rage, or who fights back. In any case, we are chosen not only because of our qualifications, but also because we fit a certain role that fits in the drama.

In an ideal and enlightened workplace, coworkers are willing to consider these issues. In less ideal situations, discussion will be blocked. In either case, we can take the opportunity to study it for ourselves and discover the cyclic drama within the workplace. In this way, we can be better prepared to work with others, understanding what is taking place, looking at the different roles people play, and discovering our own role. Others may not be willing to examine their particular place in the drama, but we can always look at our parts and learn from them. To the degree we understand our roles, we will be less likely to take them on. If we experience great difficulty in avoiding our roles, we will recognize the need for serious reflection (see Appendix II for suggestions). And if we really come to understand the nature of why we play out these roles, and their history in our lives, we will gain a freedom from them. We will be able to watch the drama unfold in the workplace, while attaining a vantage point that is free of it; in this way we will be better prepared to work with others who remain stuck in it.

An Example of a Drama and Dialogue in the Workplace

Let us consider an example of of roles and dramas that can take place in a workplace. Imagine that your manager asks you to write up a proposal to initiate a new procedure in the office. According to this procedure, you would be in charge of organizing information on a project for your coworkers. You immediately draw up the proposal and submit it, but the manager does not act on it. Consequently, disorganization continues to exist among your coworkers on the project. The manager calls you in and holds you responsible for the lack of organization. She says that you were given a responsibility. You respond by saying that you made the proposal requested, and the manager, in turn, says that the proposal is not the point at issue. Until the proposal is initiated, you are responsible for maintaining organization of the project.

In order to evaluate this kind of situation, it is important to first chart out the *events* and *stages* in the drama.

1. State of disorganization exists in the project
2. Manager asks you to make a proposal
3. You write and turn in the proposal
4. Proposal is not acted upon—disorganization continues
5. Manager calls you in and blames you for the problem of disorganization

In the second part of your evaluation, describe the states of mind that you and others went through in each scene.

1. State of disorganization exists in the project (concern, anxiousness, lack of focus and clarity among team)
2. Manager asks you to make a proposal (manager is in a very positive state of mind and supportive; you feel good, as if manager is giving you an important responsibility;

you are establishing good communication and a positive working relationship)

3. You write and turn in the proposal (you feel excited about having submitted excellent work; manager accepts it and is matter-of-fact)

4. Proposal is not acted upon—disorganization continues (you are confused and troubled and want to speak up about it; team is frustrated; manager is distant)

5. Manager calls you in and blames you for the problem of disorganization (manager is furious; you are hurt and quiet; you accept blame)

In evaluating this event as a drama, it is important to consider both the high and the low states of mind that each of the characters goes through. In this example:

1. Team is relatively low
   You are low
   Manager is neither high nor low
2. Team is still low
   You are very high
   Manager is positive
3. Team is more positive
   You are relatively high
   Manager is neither high nor low
4. Team is relatively low
   You are low
   Manager is distant
5. Team is frustrated
   You are very low
   Manager is angry, but high and filled with energy

You can then chart this drama out as a cycle, looking at its highs and lows. You will notice that the event has its own flow and dynamic. You might become aware of other scenes that have transpired in the workplace that were similar to this one. You may even remember recent and past scenes in your own life that have similarities to this scene. At this point you want to ask, "Did I act ideally in this situation?" You examine the scene and realize, "No, I didn't act ideally. I saw that the proposal was not being acted upon, and I ignored it. I should have spoken up." Moreover, in the last scene, you also see that you had a second opportunity to speak up, but instead you remained silent and took the blame.

Now you must ask yourself, "Why didn't I speak up?" This is an essential question for many reasons. For one, the entire drama might have been avoided if you had spoken up. In truth, we never know how another is going to respond. Second, this is what you saw as the best and most appropriate thing to do. "Why didn't I act upon it? What blocked me from following my clear vision of what was best?" It is likely that you are seeing that this is a problem in your life that recurs in many different situations and prevents you from doing what needs to be done. Moreover, you may see that by not speaking up, you often "take on the blame," thereby "saving" other people from their own problems.

Finally, you must ask what roles the other people around you are taking on. Why didn't the manager act on the proposal? Is it curious that she gets in a high state of mind when she gets angry? Is this in fact the only time when she seems to express any vitality or energy? It may be that she expresses herself only when she gets angry. You may also see in her a similarity to one of your parents. And how did your coworkers respond? Did they blame you and save the manager, too? Do they play a supporting role in this drama, acting like siblings?

This is an example of the kind of reflecting that we may find helpful in better understanding the dramas in our own particular workplace. Whatever the particular drama, a structure similar to the one presented in this example will be helpful. We need to see the stages, the states of mind, the dynamic, and the roles each person plays. Then we need to find a way to discuss the situation with our coworkers.

In the example given, it is necessary first to clarify what happened. Ask the manager why she did not act upon the proposal. At that point, explain that you were holding yourself back from asking the reason for the delay and were watching as the project continued to be disorganized. There may have been a number of reasons why the manager didn't act. She may have been waiting for you to push her to act. She may have been caught up in something else and held you responsible to remind her. Or she may have been sabotaging the project for some reason, which she may or may not be willing to admit or which she may not understand herself. You must decide what kind of dialogue you want to have with the manager, and this depends upon how much you are willing to risk and how much you think she will understand and appreciate. And of course, these factors are always, to some degree, completely unknown.

In an ideal situation, you will be able to discuss the problem. Say, for example, that the manager responds by saying that she was caught up in other things and that it was your responsibility to remind her. Then you have the opportunity to raise this as a question for dialogue. It is not helpful to take the position "It was not my responsibility. I handed in the proposal." Avoid this path, because by taking this position, we force the other person to defend herself by taking the opposite position, which usually leads to an argument. It will be more beneficial if you take the opportunity for dialogue and raise a good question, because when a dialogue is initiated there immediately arises a state of openness and exploration. There are no sides being taken. Dialogue initiates the opportunity for people to work together as friends in clarifying the issue. Since there is no arguing, there is no need to take on the role of a knower, and therefore there exists an openness to new possibilities.

For instance, in the previous example you could ask, "What is the role of the manager, and what is the role of the team member on this project?" By beginning the discussion with a good question, you are in a better position to discover how the manager sees the dynamics of the workplace as well as being more able to gain a better understanding of her approach to the particular issue under discussion. By appealing to this more general question, you are also better able to avoid the emotions that accompany the particular problem. This will create a spirit of dialogue that we can use as a foundation for the transition to the difficulty, and when we do make the transition we can appeal to the general principles that were discussed as a basis for addressing the particular problem. In all such situations, it is always important to recognize both roles in the drama. If you admit that you ought to have inquired into the status of the proposal, you are also, in a good position to present a challenge to her. For example, if the manager states that the role of a manager is to oversee the team, then you have a right to ask why she expects a team member (namely, yourself) to oversee her.

This gives the manager the opportunity to reflect on her role in the drama, and she, in turn, may be able to gain valuable insight into the way she relates to others. Just as you discovered your pattern of not speaking your mind and taking the blame, she may discover a pattern and role that she plays out in her life. The two of you will have transcended your roles in the workplace and will have been able to reflect together in the most meaningful way; that is the basis for a significant friendship. Keep in mind, though, that not all people are going to be willing to go forward or equally far in these kinds of dialogues. Therefore, you ought to consider how far is appropriate, given the person you are engaged in dialogue with. In the end, following this approach will lead everyone on a more fruitful path for self-reflection, even in a short discussion.

10 CREATING A DIALOGIC SOCIETY: A PRACTICAL PROPOSAL FOR EDUCATION

The creation of a dialogic society is the highest aim of a democracy. In a dialogic society, there is honest and forthright discussion of the issues and decisions facing communities and the nation following the principles of dialogue. This calls for focusing the question and issue, seeking the truth, working together as friends, and following the words. The reality of American politics is far from this ideal. Many politicians regularly violate all of these principles. In fact, quite often their very success as politicians depends upon it. The game of politics today is to create the kind of image that people, business, and the media will support. To do this, politicians often follow a set of rules, which sometimes are the very opposite of the principles of dialogue and earn the name of sophists.

The first rule of sophistry speaking is to *ignore the question* asked. The political sophist does this in order to redirect the discussion to the issue he wants to speak about. The second is to *ignore the truth*. The politician ignores the truth because his goal is to convey a very specific image to the public. Thirdly, the political sophist is *not concerned with friendship*. His only concern is the advancement of his career, which can be accomplished at the cost of his constituents, his political allies, and his country. Finally, the political sophist achieves his desired image by the conscious *misinterpretation of the words* of others and the freedom to reinterpret his own words when necessary.

There is no need to go into a detailed critique of American politics, because most Americans are aware of the fact that politicians too rarely represent the interests of the people, nor do they bring much integrity to the work they do. And, unfortunately, the system in place allows for little else. In order to have leaders with integrity, Americans must first desire to foster these same principles in their own lives. We consistently complain about our leaders, but how many of us who complain about the government would act differently if put in a position of power? If Americans truly desire to change society, we must first change ourselves.

With this change, it would be relatively easy to also change our electoral process to accommodate a desire for truth and integrity in our political process. A good deal of the problems in American politics originate in the campaign process. Politicians require millions of dollars to run their campaigns. In order to raise this money, they must seek out wealthy individuals, businesses, and political action committees. Consequently, politicians win elections based on money and effective advertising in the media and not on their capacity to work for the good of the people.

A dialogic society would not permit this. Such a society would demand that its leaders discuss the issues of the day in the most meaningful way. And it would be a very simple task to enforce such discussion. Advertising could easily be eliminated from the electoral process, and the media could be utilized to present a series of real dialogues on the campaign issues. Moreover, the electoral process could be shortened, as it is in many other democracies that seek to maintain the integrity of their elections. In the end, voters would be more likely to cast their votes based on a consideration of the words of the candidates and not necessarily on their images.

A commitment to the principles of dialogue is an important means to the kinds of changes that would bring about better individuals, communities, businesses, and leaders. The ideal of dialogue expresses simple principles that we all generally accept, and yet to put them into practice is a great challenge to individuals and society as a whole. One of the simplest ways to bring these ideals into our society is through education. The introduction of education through dialogue would literally revolutionize education. Let us present a simple example to illustrate why this would be the case.

Imagine a simple geometry lesson. In school a teacher stands before the class and presents a lecture on the subject to thirty to fifty students. Of these students, only a handful completely follow the material. The majority do not have the attention span to pay attention to a lecture. The students go home and attempt to study the material on their own and are then tested to see how well they have done. A few get As, some get Bs, most get Cs, and the rest Ds and Fs. Then the teacher moves on to the next chapter in the book. A dialogic education would function very differently. Dialogues take place between two to four people. There is no way of hiring this many teachers, nor is there such a need. The dialogues concerning the geometry lesson could be led by students who have already demonstrated an understanding of the material. Therefore, students in the grade ahead, for example, would have the responsibility of sharing their understanding with their classmates in the grade below. The teacher would supervise these dialogues and be responsible for assisting where dialogic partners get stuck. They would also test to see that the students had mastered the material. In this model, all the students would be required to get a grade of "A" because they would be responsible for sharing their understanding with others.

A school could apply this approach in a very limited way or it could be the major component of an educational program. Either method would have tremendous benefits. For one, students would become empowered. They would discover what active learning is all about. Second, students would be given an important responsibility in the learning process and discover the joy and intrinsic value and beauty of helping another learn. This would cultivate a deeper appreciation of the mind in our society. It would also demonstrate to students that they are all capable of mastering a certain amount of material, that all students have the potential for excellence.

In order to bring an entire class of students to the mastery of some material, the educational system would have to deal with the problems and blocks that particular students might experience. And so the teacher and dialogic leader would have to possess a great deal of compassion and concern for where each student is in his or her development and understanding. This would demand that education become a more human activity, which can happen only when students are able, at times, to work with others or with their teachers on a one-on-one basis. This goal can realistically be achieved only if we use other students as dialogic mentors.

In this form of education, all the students will gain a valuable lesson about communication and working together. Through this approach students necessarily build bonds of friendship, which is the necessary consequence of working together to reach understanding. Moreover, students will learn that despite their cultural or religious differences, all are able to gain the same understanding of certain fundamental ideas common to humans. Instead of competing against one another for grades, all the students work together toward a common goal and experience the intrinsic value of this kind of activity as a means of relating.

As a consequence of such an educational program, students would be naturally initiated into the principles of dialogue. There would be no need for lectures and persuasion. Students would experience for themselves what it means to focus on a question or issue, seek the truth together as friends, and go step by step following the words. Thus, they would experience the benefits of working together rather than competing against one another; and they would discover that this path toward the truth has the highest value, for when one gains understanding with another there is a true sense of satisfaction that cannot be compared to material success.

The classic model for such an education comes from Plato's dialogue called *Meno*, in which Socrates demonstrates the process of learning by leading a young aristocrat's slave through a simple geometry exercise. In the dialogue, Meno, the young aristocrat, is unwilling to admit that he does not know, but his slave is, and therefore is able to learn. This example aims to illustrate what Socrates and Plato considered to be the most important part of learning—questions. When a person listens to a lecture, she may or may not be interested in the subject. However, when one is led through ideas by questions, one is able to see the significance of important ideas and become directly connected to the process of learning. Socrates reveals in this demonstration that genuine learning occurs only when a student is able to see that she doesn't know what she thinks she knows. Only then will the student be possessed by the question and "stung," as Socrates says. Once the student appreciates the question and sees it as her own, she will continue the process of learning eagerly and joyfully. And when she is led by questions, she will be given the wonderful opportunity to come to the moment of insight and genuine learning for herself, and in that experience discover the beauty of the human mind. In *Meno* this is called the memory awakening because Socrates and other great philosophers believe that the soul is immortal and possesses all knowledge.

We leave the reader with this selection from *Meno*, the very dialogue that inspired the writing of this book. Socrates' approach to learning can be applied in many different situations. It is my sincere hope that this introduction to the art of dialogue will encourage readers to adapt the principles in ways that are appropriate to their lives, to their families and professions, and in this way help contribute to the good of our future.

> *Socrates:* Direct your mind then to this question: Which does the demonstration reveal to you to be the case—that the boy is experiencing the memory awakening or is learning from me?
> *Meno:* I will do this.
> *Socrates:* Tell me now, boy, do you recognize that a quadrangular space is this kind of thing? [Socrates draws the space in the sand.]

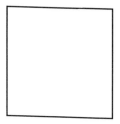

Boy: I do.

Socrates: It is then a quadrangular space since it has all of these sides equal, all four of them?

Boy: Of course.

Socrates: And it has these lines through the middle and they are equal? (Socrates draws the lines.)

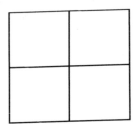

Boy: Yes.

Socrates: And wouldn't it still be the same kind of space if it were either bigger or smaller?

Boy: Of course.

Socrates: Then if this side were two feet and this one two feet, how many feet would the whole be? Consider it this way. If this side were two feet and this other side were only one foot, isn't it true that the space would be two feet taken once? (Socrates marks off such a space from the figure.)

Boy: Yes.

Socrates: And when this side and the other side are two feet, doesn't the area of the space become two feet taken twice?

Boy: It does.

Socrates: Therefore, the area becomes two feet taken twice?

Boy: Yes.

Socrates: How many then is twice two? Count and tell me.

Boy: Four, Socrates.

Socrates: Then could there be another space double the area of this one, and is this kind of space also one in which all of its lines are equal?

Boy: Yes.

Socrates: How many feet then will this space be?

Boy: Eight.

Socrates: Come now and try to tell me exactly how long each of its lines will be? The line of the other space was two feet. What then will be the length of the line of the space that is double the area of the first?

Boy: It's clear, Socrates, that it will be double.

Socrates: Do you see, Meno, I am not teaching him anything; instead I am asking him everything. And now he thinks he knows how big the line is from which the eight-foot space is formed. Or does it not appear this way to you?

Meno: No, it does.

Socrates: Then he doesn't know?

Meno: Not at all.

Socrates: But he thinks in any case it is made from the double?

Meno: Yes.

Socrates: Watch now as he goes step by step along the path of the memory awakening, in the way it is necessary for the memory to awaken. (He then speaks to the boy.) Tell me now, is it from the doubled line that you say the doubled space is formed? This is the kind of thing I mean—not a space with one side long and another short, but one having all its sides equal, just like this one, and also double in size so that it is eight feet. Now see if to you it still appears that this space will be from the line that is doubled.

Boy: It does appear so, to me at least.

Socrates: So, then, since the doubled line is formed from that one, should we add another line of the same length to it?

Boy: Of course. (Socrates adds another line to the original line and equal to it.)

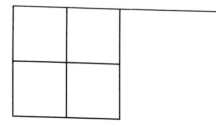

Socrates: And it is from that line, then, you say that the eight-foot space will be? So then there should be four of them?

Boy: Yes.

Socrates: Let us then, starting from this line, draw out four equal lines. (Socrates draws out the square built from the doubled line.)

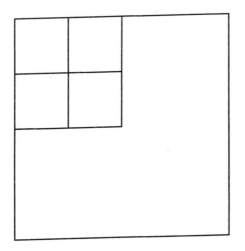

Socrates: Isn't this, therefore, what you would say an eight-foot space is?

Boy: Of course.

Socrates: And within this space, aren't there four spaces, each of which is equal to the four-foot space?

Boy: Yes.

Socrates: How big then will it be? Won't it be four times as great as the original space?

Boy: How could it be otherwise?

Socrates: Is then the quadrupled space the double?

Boy: By Zeus, no.

Socrates: How much greater is it than the original space?

Boy: Four times as great.

Socrates: From the line that is doubled, therefore, my boy, not a doubled but a quadrupled space is formed.

Boy: That's true.

Socrates: Because four taken four times is sixteen, isn't it?

Boy: Yes.

Socrates: The eight-foot space comes from which line then? Not from a line of the quadrupled space?

Boy: I agree.

Socrates: And the four-foot space comes from a line that is half of this line there? (Socrates points to the doubled line of the quadrupled space.)

Boy: Yes.

Socrates: So it does. The eight-foot space doesn't come from the doubled line, on the one hand, nor, on the other hand, from half of it? Neither, then, will it come from a line greater than one that is this big (he points to the doubled line), nor from one that is less than this one (he points to the original two-foot line), or do you disagree?

Boy: To me it appears this way.

Socrates: Good. Since they appear this way, answer this. Tell me, wasn't this line two feet and this one four?

Boy: Yes.

Socrates: So the line of the eight-foot space must be bigger than this two-foot line, but less than the four-foot line?

Boy: It must.

Socrates: Try, then, to say how long it is.

Boy: Three feet.

Socrates: Then for the line to be three feet, we will extend it by half of this line (the two-foot line) and it will be three feet? For this is two feet, and half of it is one. (Socrates extends the line.) And from here in the same way; this is two feet, and half of it is one. And it becomes the space of which you speak?

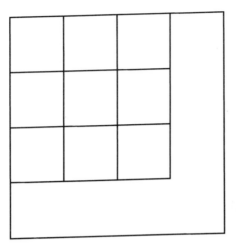

Boy: Yes.

Socrates: Then if one side is three and the other side is three, the whole space is three feet taken three times?

Boy: It seems so.

Socrates: And how many feet is three taken three times?

Boy: Nine.

Socrates: But it was necessary for the double to be how many feet?

Boy: Eight.

Socrates: Neither then from the three-foot line can the eight-foot space be made.

Boy: Certainly not.

Socrates: But then from what kind of line? Try to tell us precisely. And if you don't wish to answer in numbers, show us the kind of line from which it comes.

Boy: But by Zeus, Socrates, I really do not know.

Socrates: Do you have in mind now, Meno, to where it is he has already proceeded along the path on which the memory is awakened? That at first he did not know from which line the eight-square-foot space was formed, as indeed now he still doesn't know. But he did think at that moment that he knew, and he boldly answered as if he knew and did not suppose he was at a loss. Now, though, he does suppose he is at a loss. And as, indeed, he doesn't know, neither does he think he knows.

Meno: That is true.

Socrates: And so is he now better off in regard to that which he didn't know?

Meno: This also appears right to me.

Socrates: Then by making him be at a loss and numb, as the stingray does, have we harmed him at all?

Meno: No, to me it doesn't appear so.

Socrates: This is because we have prepared him, as it looks, to discover how this question is answered. For now he will search, and he will do it gladly, since he is in a state of not knowing. Whereas before, he thought he could go before large audiences and on numerous occasions speak quite well and with ease about the doubled space and how it must be formed from the line that is double in length of the figure that is going to be doubled.

Meno: It looks that way.

Socrates: Do you think that he would have tried to seek or learn what he thought he knew, but didn't, before he fell down into the state of being at a loss, concluded he didn't know, and then desired to have what he lacked?

Meno: It doesn't appear to me he would have, Socrates.

Socrates: Therefore, he benefited by the stinging and benumbing?

Meno: It appears so to me.

Socrates: Consider now: from out of this state of being at a loss, he will discover the answer searching for it with me. And I shall be doing nothing but asking questions, nor will I be teaching him. Be on guard, though, should you discover me somewhere teaching and expounding my opinions rather than questioning him about his opinions. (He then speaks to the boy.) So tell me, isn't this our four-foot space? Do you understand?

Boy: I do.

Socrates: Can we add another to it, this one that is equal?

Boy: Yes.

Socrates: And a third, this one here, equal to each of the others?

Boy: Yes.

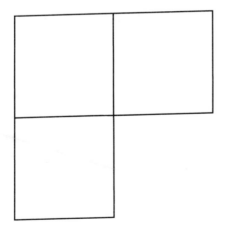

Socrates: And then can we add this one here in the corner to complete it?

Boy: Of course.

161

Socrates: Hasn't it become four equal spaces, this figure here?

Boy: Yes.

Socrates: Now then, how many times greater has the whole become than this? (Socrates points to the original space.)

Boy: Four times.

Socrates: And we were required to form the double? Or don't you remember?

Boy: Of course.

Socrates: And then is it possible for this line extended from corner to corner to cut each of the spaces in half?

Boy: Yes.

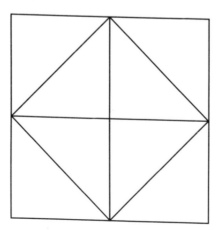

Socrates: And these four lines that are formed are all equal, the ones that embrace this space?

Boy: They are equal.

Socrates: Examine it for yourself now.

Boy: I don't understand.

Socrates: Aren't there four of these spaces, and hasn't each line cut each of the spaces in half?

Boy: Yes.

Socrates: How many of these [four-foot spaces] are in this? (Socrates points to the quadrupled space.)

Boy: Four.

Socrates: How many in this one? (Socrates points to the space that he has just formed within the quadrupled space.)

Boy: Two.

Socrates: And what is the relation of four to two?

Boy: Double.

Socrates: How many feet is this one?

Boy: Eight.

Socrates: From which line?

Boy: From this one.

Socrates: From the one that extends from corner to corner in the four-foot spaces?

Boy: Yes.

Socrates: The wise men call this the diagonal. So, then, if the name of this line is the diagonal, it would be from the diagonal, as you say, slave of Meno, that the double space is formed.

Boy: It certainly would, Socrates.

Socrates: What do you say, Meno? Does it appear to you that any of the opinions the boy gave were not from himself?

Meno: No, the answers were from himself.

Socrates: And yet he did not know, as we were saying just before.

Meno: That's true.

Socrates: So they were existing within him, these opinions, or not?

Meno: Yes, they were.

Socrates: For one who doesn't know, therefore, about the things he does not know, there exist within true opinions about those things of which he doesn't know.

Meno: It seems so.

Socrates: And now, like a dream, these opinions are being stirred in him. And so, if someone will continue questioning him about these same things often and in many ways, you know that when he completes this process, he will know about these things as accurately as anyone.

Meno: That's likely.

Socrates: Won't he then know these things not because of any teaching, but from questioning and regaining the knowledge himself from out of himself?

Meno: Yes.

Socrates: Isn't the regaining by oneself of knowledge within oneself the awakening of the memory?

Meno: Of course.

TOOLS FOR CRITICAL REASONING

Principles of Good and Bad Reasoning Simplified

The set of rules that governs good and bad arguments is called logic. Logic is to argumentation as grammar is to language. The interesting thing about language is that whether or not a speaker of a language studies the grammar formally, every speaker gains a working understanding of the rules that govern the formation of good sentences. We gain this by hearing and reading our native language (or a foreign language we are studying) consistently and by being corrected by other speakers when we misuse the language. It is therefore an organic process by which we gain mastery of a language. (It is organic in the sense that the mastery does not come from the conscious memorization of rules but from the actual practice and use of the language.) Grammar is an attempt to articulate and formalize in a system the rules that govern language, but no speaker consciously appeals to any such formal system. Speakers of a language have a direct knowledge of the language as a whole that allows them to function effortlessly, freely, fluidly, and immediately, for the activity of understanding or forming sentences happens instantaneously. This ability is called mastery.

The principles required for good reasoning also have an organic quality and can be mastered. The reason we do not have the mastery of reasoning that we have of language is because we do not live in a culture that is fluent in good reasoning. If we lived among people who constantly read mathematics and philosophy and discussed ideas in a way governed by good reasoning, we could become fluent in this world too. In many ways, the philosophical circles of the ancient Greek world sought to establish this kind of fluency through the practice of dialectic. However, since we don't live in such a world, it is a little more difficult to gain this understanding. All the same, it is important to preserve the organic quality of the subject. Whereas it is vital to study the principles of the grammar of a foreign language, we all know that the best way to learn a language is to use it. In the same way, it is important to understand the basic principles of good and bad reasoning, but the most important thing to do is to practice good reasoning in dialogue. With this in mind, we shall present a brief outline of these principles.

The goal of reasoning is simply to establish conclusions that follow appropriately from premises that are true. Our society has come to place a great deal of trust in logic, as if logic were the key to truth. However, logic is simply a structure and can just as easily be used to express falsehoods or nonsensical statements. For example, one of the most important principles in logic is called *modus ponens,* or affirming the antecedent. It is a structure that shows when it is valid in an argument to draw a certain conclusion.

If A is true, then B is true.
A is true.
Therefore, B is true.

We can use this structure in the following argument:

If I water the plants, the plants will grow.
I watered the plants.
Therefore, the plants will grow.

However, just because I present my reasoning in a valid structure does not necessarily mean that my conclusion is true. The argument assumes that besides watering them, I give them sun, proper soil, and infinite other requirements. In reasoning we generally assume all those other things. However, the best kind of reasoning tries to articulate in some respect what the assumption is. For example, one can say, "If I water the plants, the plants will grow, assuming I do everything else that is necessary." One of the limitations of logic is that it can never articulate all the necessary conditions for truth, unless it restricts truth to a system, as do calculators or computers.

The other main limitation of logic is the fact that every logical argument must assume the truth of its premises in order to justify the conclusion. All logical arguments are therefore based on an implicit "if" qualification and are therefore all hypothetical. In this respect, an argument is only as true as its premises. We can have an argument expressed in a valid structure, like the example given, but that only makes it logical. It does not make it true. The truth of a valid argument depends upon the truth of its premises.

Consequently, we are able to assume anything (whether it is true or false) and place these statements within a valid logical structure. For example:

> If birds can fly, then the moon is made of cheese.
> Birds can fly.
> Therefore, the moon is made of cheese.

Well, this is obviously a false conclusion, but it is presented in the form of a valid argument, that is, a valid structure.

Logic is something that can help one become a more precise reasoner, but a thorough understanding of systematic logic is not essential to becoming a good reasoner any more than it is essential for a great writer to be a grammarian. What is essential, though, is to understand the essence of good reasoning. A good start toward this understanding is mastering the structure of Euclid, as outlined earlier, and mastering the concepts just explained. What is also essential is to understand what guidelines exist for bad or fallacious reasoning.

Logicians have established rules for the formation of valid arguments, but it is perhaps more helpful to understand what makes an argument fallacious. Fallacies can be broken up into three major categories.

1. The Fallacy of Inconsistency

This fallacy is committed when a speaker expresses two statements that are contradictory, that is, they both cannot be true. In a well-reasoned argument, it must be possible for one's premises and conclusion to all be true.

2. The Fallacy of Circular Reasoning

This fallacy is committed when a speaker uses premises to support a conclusion that do not differ from the very conclusion that he or she is aiming to support. In a well-reasoned argument, a reason for a conclusion must be different from the conclusion. For example, if a student asks a teacher why he or she received an F on a paper and the teacher replies, "Because it is an F paper," that is circular reasoning. The explanation of the teacher's conclusion (the F grade) does not differ from the conclusion and therefore adds nothing to account for or explain it.

3. The Fallacy of Unwarranted Assumptions

This is the fallacy called a *non sequitur,* which in Latin means "It does not follow." This fallacy is committed when a speaker presents premises that fail to provide sufficient reasoning for one's conclusion. A reasoner can make this mistake by using vague or ambiguous language, false patterns of reasoning, an appeal to insufficient evidence, or an appeal to irrelevant matters, such as emotions, popular prejudice, or personal criticisms. These are all fallacies, because the nature of good reasoning is to give reasons that support one's conclusion.

As we can see, each of these kinds of non sequiturs can also be the basis for very effective rhetoric. Rhetoric literally means "persuasive speaking." One can be persuasive through good reasoning or by means of fallacies. Rhetoric is most often used to describe those who have taken the latter approach. By becoming more aware of false reasoning, one can better recognize when someone is employing this false rhetoric and be better able to name the rhetorical trick that the rhetorician is employing and explain why it is fallacious. The reader may find it meaningful to further explore the issue of fallacies in any good textbook on critical thinking.

It is especially important to become familiar with all the varieties of fallacies and their Latin names when one is functioning in the competitive arena of debates or law courts. A dialogue, though, is very different. In a dialogue the speakers do not usually set out to prove a conclusion. Instead, they present their views or judgments on an issue and the reasons why they believe their judgments to be true. Since the dialogists proceed together in the exploration, they will naturally evaluate the forms of reasoning and will likely agree on what is a good or poor reason for a certain judgment, if they are both honest and friendly in their exploration. Therefore, many of these issues can emerge more organically if the dialogists seek to express the nature of their reasoning in words. Since it is a friendly exploration, there is no need for formal and systematized rules. The principles of reasoning in a dialogue will naturally emerge from the honest and sincere discussion.

Euclid's Model of a Geometrical Proposition

The foundation for Euclid's proofs are a set of *definitions* of the geometrical objects he discusses; a set of *postulates*, which are procedures and principles specific to his subject, that is, geometry; and a set of *common notions*, which are principles of reasoning common to all subjects of knowledge. We will take a look at Proposition 1, the first geometrical proof in his *Elements of Geometry*, which appeals to the following starting points. (It also appeals to a number of other definitions indirectly, since the definitions build upon one another. The interested reader is encouraged to examine Euclid's text.)

Postulate 1: To draw a straight line from any point to any point.

Postulate 3: To describe a circle with any center and distance.

Definition 15: A circle is a plane figure such that all the straight lines falling upon it from one point among those lying within the circle are equal to one another.

Common Notion 1: Things that are equal to the same thing are also equal to one another.

The propositions are presented according to a very specific structure, which we will see is an excellent model for any kind of presentation. A complete proposition consists of six parts:

1. An *enunciation* states that which is given and that which is sought.
2. An *exposition* takes separately that which is given and prepares it in advance for use in the investigation.
3. A *specification* takes separately that which is sought and makes clear precisely what it is.
4. A *construction* adds that which is lacking in the given for finding that which is sought.
5. A *proof* draws out the reasoning to establish that which is sought from that which has been admitted.
6. A *conclusion* reverts to the enunciation and confirms that which has been proved.

We can see that this kind of structure is ideal for any kind of presentation. For in any presentation, we ought to begin by introducing the context or background and the aim (what is *sought*) of the presentation. Then we might consider the background issues (the *given*) in themselves. Then it is helpful to make clear the goal. At this point it is essential that we provide the facts, data, charts, and so on, that provide the basis for our position, thesis, or proposal (the *construction*). Once this material is on the table, we can proceed to reason out the support for our thesis (the *proof*). And it is always important to present a *conclusion* that brings together everything we have done and show that what we sought to do has been accomplished. This structure is the basis for science, law, and business and can be used in a less formal context as well. By following this kind of structure, we ensure that we take everything step-by-step in a thorough manner.

As you go through Proposition 1, draw it out for yourself. Put it in your own words if you like (you may discover that Euclid uses language in a somewhat technical manner and labels his construction in a way that may confuse you at first), but then go back to Euclid's words and make sure you understand the proposition in his own terms as well, for they are the key to his system. (You may also enjoy trying to figure out why he chooses to name his figures in the way that he does and how that relates to the presentation.)

In order to test yourself, make sure you understand why each step is necessary to the whole process. (It is my own experience with myself and students that we reach a point where we think we understand, when in truth we have only partly understood.) In reading this book, you will see that Euclid presents every step and proceeds with clarity and precision. When you are finished, it is important that you try to share your understanding with another. This will be the true test of your own understanding. Be prepared to answer any questions that the individual with whom you discuss it may have.

Let us look at Euclid's first proposition. The parts are labeled according to the outline I have charted.

Euclid's First Proposition

ENUNCIATION
On a given finite straight line to construct an equilateral triangle.

EXPOSITION
Let AB be the given finite straight line.

SPECIFICATION
Thus it is required to construct an equilateral triangle on the straight line AB.

CONSTRUCTION

With center A and distance AB, let the circle BCD be described [Postulate 3]; again, with center B and distance BA, let the circle ACE be described [Postulate 3]; and from the point C, in which the circles cut each other, to the points A, B, let the straight lines CA, CB be joined [Postulate 1].

PROOF

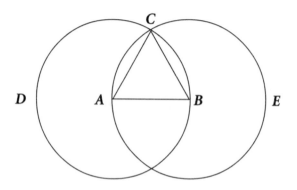

Since the point A is the center of the circle CDB, AC is equal to AB [Definition 15]. Again, since the point B is the center of the circle CAE, BC is equal to BA (BA is just a different way of naming AB from the perspective of the other circle) [Definition 15]. But CA was also proved to be equal to AB; therefore, each of the straight lines CA, CB is equal to AB. And things that are equal to the same thing are also equal to one another; therefore, CA is also equal to CB [Common Notion 1]. Therefore, the three straight lines CA, AB, BC are equal to one another.

CONCLUSION

Therefore, the triangle ABC is equilateral and it has been constructed on the given finite straight line AB. This is what it was required to do.

The Dialectic

The dialectic is a formal approach to the exploration of philosophical ideas and seeks to be exhaustive in its investigation. The dialectic is the way in which ancient philosophers used reason to develop and explore the relationships of the key terms in their philosophical picture of existence in the field of philosophy known as metaphysics. This structure is a powerful means for exploring important issues and can be used in seeking the truth of anything. In this section, I introduce a way of using the dialectical method as a basis for examining positions in a dialogue. (For those interested in dialectic in ancient philosophy, the two prime sources are Plato's *Parmenides* and Proclus's *Commentary on Plato's Parmenides*, see chapter 5.)

The dialectic can be used in its most complete form or in a more abbreviated form, depending upon our goals and time limitations. According to Parmenides, the master dialectician of the ancient Greek world, we must investigate not only what follows each time we make a hypothesis but also what follows if the hypothesis is not true. First we shall consider Parmenides' explanation of this method and then a practical approach to applying it. Parmenides explains the dialectic briefly in the following way:

> In brief, whatever the subject of your hypothesis, if you suppose that it is or is not, or that it experiences any other affection, you must consider what happens to it and to any other particular things you may choose, and to a greater number and to all in the same way. And you must consider other things in relation to themselves and to anything else you may choose in any instance, whether you suppose that the subject of your hypothesis exists or does not exist, if you are to train yourself completely to see the truth perfectly. *

The key to the dialectic is the exploration of all that follows from a position both if it is true and if it is not true. By considering a

---

* *Plato, Volume IV;* translated by H. N. Fowler (Cambridge: Harvard University, 1992), p. 233.

position or issue from both sides, we are afforded a more complete vantage point that allows us to investigate the issue much more thoroughly. Moreover, it is often essential to consider whether something *is* the case or *is not* the case. A simple example can demonstrate the importance of this approach to reasoning.

Say, for example, your car won't start. Your first hypothesis might be "My battery is dead." And so you buy a new battery and install it. But you discover the car still won't start. Rather than act on this incomplete investigation of the issue, you could have asked, "If it is not my battery, then what follows?" By considering the issue in a dialectical way— both if a failed battery is the cause and if it is not the cause—the reasoner can discover other possibilities. For example, "It might be my ignition or even a fuse." Well, a bad fuse is the simplest and cheapest possible answer, so you might try replacing the fuse and discover that this corrects the problem. Thus, if we take the dialectical approach and consider the hypothesis in two ways, (1) if the dead battery is the cause of the car not starting, and (2) if a dead battery is not the cause, we can have a much clearer view of the issue and, in the example presented, can save ourselves the price of a new battery.

In order to see the truth of an issue perfectly, we must consider the issue in a systematic and complete fashion called the dialectic. The ancient philosopher Proclus presented a model of the formal outline of a dialectical examination (there is both a short form and a long form). The dialectic works by considering a hypothetical position and what follows in terms of something that is affected by the hypothesis. For example, take the case of a professional woman who has two children and is offered a certain job opportunity. The woman has a difficult decision to make, because her choice will affect her life, her relationship with her husband, and her children. In such a circumstance, it is important to look at the issue in a very thorough manner. We often do this in a simple way by considering the pros and cons. The dialectic is a way of exploring the pros and cons, but it also charts them out with respect to how the issue affects those involved. In our example, the hypothesis is "If she takes the job." The woman must consider what follows for those involved.

She can consider first how it affects her children and, second, what follows for her husband. Or she may choose to contemplate what results for her family as a whole. The dialectic can be used to explore the hypothetical path in relationship to anything that is affected by the choice. And, of course, the dialectic method looks at the issue both if the hypothetical path is taken and if it is not taken. Simply put, the dialectic is a structure by which to consider systematically the pros and cons, the relationships involved, and the positive and negative cases of the hypothetical path. The dialectical method can be the basis for a dialogue where one party takes on the questioner role and draws out the implications of the position being considered and the other player simply answers.

If Monique takes the job offer, what follows for Monique
    1. in relation to herself?
    2. in relation to her children?

If Monique takes the job offer, what follows for her children
    3. in relation to Monique?
    4. in relation to themselves?

If Monique does not accept the job offer, what follows for Monique
    5. in relation to herself?
    6. in relation to her children?

If Monique does not accept the job offer, what follows for her children
    7. in relation to Monique?
    8. in relation to themselves?

It is likely that there will be some degree of repetition in one's answers, especially with regard to the complementary questions in their positive and negative forms. The things that follow for Monique in relation to herself in the first question will also be appropriate answers to the fifth question, but with the hypothesis negated. If she takes the job, she will make more money. If she doesn't take the job, she won't make more money. If she takes the job, she will have less free time. If she doesn't take the job, she will have more free time. Seeing these issues expressed both positively and negatively gives one a more objective perspective on the issue. Also, it will allow you to exercise your mind about the issue, which will prepare the conditions for deeper insight into the true good. Don't be hesitant to repeat the same points in both their positive and negative forms, and you will see that by doing so you will also discover important implications not previously evident.

Dialectic—The Short Form

The dialectic can be used for any issue, person, relationship, business, entity, or idea. Here is the dialectic in its abstract form.

If X follows a certain position or path, what follows for X
    1. in relation to itself?
    2. in relation to the other?

If X follows a certain position or path, what follows for the other
    3. in relationship to X?
    4. in relationship to itself?

If X does not follow a certain position or path, what follows for X
    5. in relation to the X?
    6. in relation to to other?

If X does not follow a certain position or path, what follows for the other
    7. in relationship to X?
    8. in relationship to itself?

In applying the dialectic to the exploration of ideas, we would consider the hypothesis that something is true and then consider what follows for something else. So, for example: "If drugs are legalized, what follows for those who are addicted to drugs?"

Dialectic—The Long Form

There is also a long form of the dialectic that adds a level of complexity and thoroughness. The eight categories are expanded to twenty-four. The long form also adds the category of what follows and does not follow, which allows for those kinds of things that are true in one sense, yet not true in another. For example, if Monique takes the job offer, it both follows and does not follow in relation to herself that she will be more fulfilled in her life. That is, she will be more fulfilled in her life as a professional but not more fulfilled in her life as a mother.

If X follows a certain position or path
1. what follows in relation to itself?
2. what does not follow in relation to itself?
3. what both follows and does not follow in relation to itself?
4. what follows for it in relation to the other?
5. what does not follow for it in relation to the other?
6. what follows and does not follow for it in relation to the other?
7. what follows for the other in relation to itself?
8. what does not follow for the other in relation to itself?
9. what follows and does not follow for the other in relation to itself?
10. what follows for the other in relation to it?
11. what does not follow for the other in relation to it?
12. what both follows and does not follow for the other in relation to it?

If X does not follow a certain position or path
13. what follows in relation to itself?
14. what does not follow in relation to itself?
15. what both follows and does not follow in relation to itself?
16. what follows for it in relation to the other?

17. what does not follow for it in relation to the other?
18. what follows and does not follow for it in relation to the other?
19. what follows for the other in relation to itself?
20. what does not follow for the other in relation to itself?
21. what follows and does not follow for the other in relation to itself?
22. what follows for the other in relation to it?
23. what does not follow for the other in relation to it?
24. what both follows and does not follow for the other in relation to it?

The goal of the dialectic is to draw out as much of the pertinent information and the relationships involved so that the issue can be seen most completely and clearly. Many issues are, of course, very complicated, and this way of unfolding the nature of the issue can help exercise the mind in a focused way about all the relationships concerned. It may also help bring to light implications that were unnoticed and therefore unforeseen. This method, then, can be the basis for a dialogue in which one party takes on the questioner role and draws out the implications and the other simply answers.

Once the information is outlined, it is an essential task to establish a hierarchy of priorities. What are the most important factors that need to be taken into consideration in making the decision? Here the critical issue is what the most important goals are. And does the accomplishment of one set of goals outweigh others? Is there a way to achieve all your goals simultaneously? Do some goals require the accomplishment of others? In our example, it is clear that different families will have different views on what is considered most important. Some families may consider their children above everything. Others may consider their own professional lives as most important. In order to bring all the pieces together, it is always essential to keep in mind the greater whole.

Holistic Contrasted with Analytic Thinking

The essential concern in dialectic is the relationship between wholes and parts. In any issue there is going to be the question of the relationship between the whole and the parts. We live in a culture that has historically isolated parts from wholes, and we are just beginning to see the dangerous implications of this way of thinking. This approach is called analytic thinking. When we seek medical advice, we often go to a specialist, who focuses on one part of the body. But when the body is ill, can it be healed by separating one part from the whole? Is the problem isolated, or is it that the problem appears to be manifesting in an isolated part? The Greek art of healing held the view that the body could not be healed in parts but must be considered as one entity. Moreover, they believed that the ultimate cause of all illness is not in the body but in the psyche of the individual (the Greeks use the term *psyche* for what we generally call the individual mind); therefore, true healing must address the psyche. This is the genuine form of holistic healing.

No matter what our view on health matters, the point is that in exploring any issue, it is essential to discover and understand the greater whole with which our particular issue is concerned. By looking toward the whole, we find the ultimate standard and measure of what we are seeking to benefit. For example, in the case of a sick person, the goal of healing is not just to restore physical health but also to address the nature of the problem affecting the person's very life, that is, the psyche. For in truth, the psyche is the cause of the illness. By solving the physical illness, we deal with a mere part and not with the whole nor with the ultimate cause of the problem. In the end, our bodies may be temporarily healed, but the ultimate goal is to achieve a state of well-being that is accomplished only by addressing the psyche.

In any issue, it is essential to ask the following question: *What is the whole that is being affected?* This whole is the standard by which we must measure our goals. In the example of the mother and her family, the ultimate standard of an appropriate goal is the whole of which the mother and the children and husband are all parts, that is, the family. In deciding, the mother must consider not what is best for her life as an individual, but rather what is best for the family as a whole. Accordingly, what is most important is not the greatest good for any of the parts, but what most benefits the whole. Sometimes this will mean taking the job, and at other times it will mean refusing it. Ideally, of course, each member of a family would take on the goal of the family's good, so there would be no ultimate conflict between the individual and the family, the part and the whole.

At present, our society is focused on the individual, and as a consequence there have been disastrous effects upon the greater wholes of our world, whether they be families, communities, our environment, the human race, or the earth itself. Parents abandon the needs of their children, people and businesses look toward short-term profit rather than the long-term needs of their society and community, and the country itself seeks its own benefit over the good of the planet. The consequences of this kind of thinking gravely threaten our existence as a species. The dialectical approach, on the other hand, recognizes that the true good rests with the wholes, for it sees that parts gain their existence in relationship to these larger wholes.

Simile, Analogy, and Allegory

One of the most helpful tools in the communication, expression, and exploration of ideas is the use of images. These images can be expressed in terms of three related structures: similes, analogies, and allegories. A *simile* is a figure of speech that compares two things and introduces the comparison with the words *like* or *as*. "She is *like* a rose" is a simile. Similes are different than *metaphors*, which do not use *like* or *as*; for example, "she *is* a rose." In similes, the speaker draws a likeness or similitude that is like the very thing being discussed. Similes are rich literary devices that add great depth to the beauty of expression. The use of similes is central to Homer's style. One of his greatest similes concerns the anger of Achilles, which "is as sweet as slow-dripping honey." The power of similes can also bring greater clarity to our communication.

Similes are powerful means of expression because they relate a subject that is less known or more difficult to express to something that is more particular and therefore more easily understood and grasped. Anger is familiar to all of us, but it is often challenging to express our relationship to our anger and the quality of it in a literal way. Homer's simile gives us a vivid image, presenting anger as a state that we don't want to let go of, and doing so describes anger much more powerfully than any literal expression could.

In dialogue the use of likenesses is often essential to the communication of a subject. For when we use likenesses in a systematic way, we are able to make very complicated issues much simpler. For example, we may not understand the deficit issue in national economics, but we do understand balancing a checkbook. If a speaker says that national economics is like balancing a checkbook, he is obligated to explain the likeness. In explaining the likeness, the speaker will establish a set of similes: the national deficit is like personal debt, national borrowing is like a personal credit line, the national budget is like personal expenses, and so on. In all these similes the speaker moves away from a concept that is lesser known and into an area that is more familiar, thus making the ideas more easily understandable. In the discussion the speaker will focus on the likeness between the two terms, but it is also helpful and sometimes necessary to explain the differences.

Whereas similes compare the likeness between two terms, an analogy is used to express the likeness between two sets of terms. Using our previous example, we can arrange the first two relationships into an analogy by saying, national borrowing is to the national deficit as the use of personal credit is to personal debt. A four-term analogy takes the following form: A is to B as C is to D. A, B, C, and D are the four terms. A is to B and C is to D are the two ratios. The ratios express the relationships between the terms. An analogy compares the relationships between the two ratios. In other words, analogies compare relationships, not terms.

A simple analogy states: *Shepherd is to sheep as ruler is to subject.* Shepherds, of course, *feed, protect,* and *care* for their sheep. Similarly, rulers also *feed, protect,* and *care* for their subjects. Thus, it is a good analogy because it expresses this similarity. However, shepherds also shear their sheep. Rulers do not do this, but this fact does not spoil the analogy. In every analogy there are going to be things that are similar and things that are dissimilar. An analogy does not claim that the relationships are the same, only similar.

Contained within the analogy just given is the simile a *ruler is like a shepherd*. As we can see, similes can be discovered in analogies. Thus, when one uses a simile, it presupposes the structure of analogy, which organizes the larger picture from which the simile is derived. Thus, by looking for this larger picture, or drawing it out through questions in a dialogue, dialogists are able to discover the broader image they have in mind when reasoning upon an issue. For it is often the case that our opinions exist within us in the form of pictures. As is frequently said, a picture is worth a thousand words, because a single picture can contain in a simple unity a great number of relationships amongst the particulars. Reasoning through analogies allows us to unfold the implicit structure of the pictures that encapsulize our beliefs and opinions about the world—beliefs we may not have ever realized we hold, since we have never before put them into words. (This is the structure behind the idea of the *pathologos*, which we shall discuss in Appendix II.) Once we put our beliefs into words and in the structure of analogies, we are able to see whether the analogies are sound, that is, if there is a genuine likeness being expressed. Analogies are rational structures and so are easily evaluated. For an analogy to be true, the relationships between the two pairs of terms have to be similar. If they are not, the analogy must be fixed or rejected.

Analogies, like similes, also allow us to take a discussion from the less known to the more known. This can be especially helpful when misunderstanding or anger or other such emotions hinder a discussion. Analogies allow dialogists to move away from the controversial issue while, at the same time, maintain the structure of the discussion in a different and noncontroversial set of terms that preserve the relationships of the original discussion. Consider a dialogue about national politics and the issue of the deficit and social spending. If the dialogists encounter difficulty in keeping their tempers during the discussion, one of them can suggest that they speak about the national budget as if it were an individual family's budget. By redirecting their minds toward the analogous situation, they can liberate themselves temporarily from the difficulty. Moreover, the analogy allows them to express a complicated issue more simply. And since we are all more familiar with and better understand the nature of a family's budget and a family's needs, by using the terms of a family to represent the government, the dialogists can gain a clearer perspective on the issues and more clearly articulate their own positions. Many times, specific points that one has difficulty communicating are readily made clear when the discussion moves to the analogous situation.

Analogies can take various forms. There are three-term analogies (A is to B just as B is to C), four-term analogies, and extended analogies (A is to B just as C is to D . . . just as P is to Q just as R is to S). When we take the meaning expressed by the first set of terms and make a story to describe the relations in another set of terms, we form *allegories*. Allegories are stories expressed in one set of terms, but whose meaning must be discovered in separate and parallel sets of terms. Allegories differ from parables in that allegories include the parallel meaning and reveal the meaning of the story, whereas parables keep it hidden (as Jesus does in the Gospel of Mark).

Expressing meaning in an allegory adds another level of richness to this kind of image-making. Through allegories, speakers and authors can put into words the dynamics of the relationships expressed in the analogies. The most famous of all allegories is Plato's allegory of the cave, from the seventh book of the *Republic*. In it Plato characterizes the path toward enlightenment by likening it to the liberation from a life in which shadows in a cave are accepted as real to the experience of the upper world and the light of the sun.

Allegories have the ability to bring together very complex ideas in a simple and most memorable way. The mere act of trying to put our thoughts in the form of an allegory is an exercise that will allow us to see our ideas more clearly. Many people often find it much easier to deal with difficult personal issues by expressing them in a different set of terms, terms that allow them to gain a greater objectivity in looking at the issues.

PHILOSOPHICAL MIDWIFERY FOR PERSONAL GROWTH

In this appendix I present readers with a means to reflect on their own dramas and fate through the method developed by the contemporary Socratic philosopher Dr. Pierre Grimes. In the selection from Plato's *Theaetetus* previously given in the second chapter, Socrates explains that he is a kind of midwife in that he helps people bring to birth what is pregnant within their minds. We can therefore call Socrates a philosophical midwife. What is most distinctive about the role of a philosophical midwife is that he functions, unlike those who practice other arts (in a state of not knowing). This is because the midwife's role is not to convey knowledge to another but to raise questions that stir others to discover the insight they possess within themselves. However, the pregnant party may be pregnant with a falsehood. In this case, it is the midwife's role to help the person see that, indeed, the birth is false.

Although Socrates was the greatest philosopher of the ancient world, the practice of a genuine Socratic philosophy or midwifery has not been preserved in the West, and consequently it is not known in our culture. What is called the Socratic method today is merely an adaptation of a means of questioning within a traditional teaching context. The goal of a teacher who uses the Socratic method is to spur students to think and play an active role in the acquisition of information. The goal of Socratic midwifery is the growth and development of the human soul in pursuit of wisdom and excellence. Whereas modern education seeks to *inform* students, Socrates, as Grimes says, sought to *transform* them. In the spirit of Prometheus, Dr. Grimes has brought to birth an art that may provide the greatest benefit to contemporary humankind. He has reawakened the ancient Greek philosophical tradition as a living practice by using the principles of Socratic philosophy as a means for personal growth.

Dr. Grimes developed his version of philosophical midwifery not from a theoretical basis but from his own practical experience in applying Socratic questioning in counseling sessions with thousands of people over more than thirty years. His understanding of midwifery emerged as a description of the principles that have guided people toward profound insight into their personal lives.

For those who are seeking to learn about philosophical midwifery a description must be secondary. What is most important is the experience of insight into which this form of Socratic questioning leads a person. Rather than presenting a theory of midwifery, it would be more appropriate at this time to let the reader go through the process and draw her own conclusions from what she experiences and realizes. In this way, the conclusions would not be beliefs just accepted from some authority. Moreover, this method would give the reader the opportunity to explore the questions that arise from self-reflection and insight. A few introductory remarks, though, are essential.

Philosophical midwifery is a means of questioning that is used to help us resolve and understand the blocks and difficulties we encounter when we are pursuing meaningful goals. Philosophical midwifery limits explorations to this context because it provides the structure within which we can evaluate and judge the exploration. Our goals are the standard by which we can judge our growth. We know when we reach insight and understanding in midwifery because it helps us move beyond a problem that blocked us from furthering our pursuit of a goal. In midwifery a goal is defined as something we consider personally meaningful and that has stages that are required for its accomplishment. It is essential that the goal have stages because then we can identify at what stage we are, where we are blocked, and what we need to do to move closer to the goal.

Midwifery is used when we as individuals recognize that they are blocked in our pursuit of a goal. Our account of this block is called a *problem*. According to Dr. Grimes, these are the signs of a problem (one or more will signal the existence of a problem):

> Not striving for our most personally meaningful goals
> The failure to achieve our goals with excellence
> Setting secondary goals as primary
> Making practical issues the main or significant goals
> Letting opportunities go by, sabotaging opportunities for success
> Not preparing adequately for goals through loss of concentration and energy, inability to resist distractions, blaming others, or using excuses
> Being unable to maintain the goal
> Functioning ideally in crises but experiencing stress and anxiety before and after such events

In philosophical midwifery, unlike in ordinary language, a *problem* is distinguished from a *difficulty*. If we have a goal to finish a project for work and do not do it because we feel lazy, this is a difficulty. It is natural to experience difficulties in the pursuit of a goal. Merely because we feel a certain way—lazy, for instance—does not prevent us from continuing to pursue the goal. We often feel lazy before beginning a project and gain energy in the activity.

However, if we believe "I am lazy. I can't do this" and accept this belief, and if the belief causes a state of mind that blocks us from continuing the project at a specific stage in the process, then we have a problem. In midwifery the root of a problem is a false belief that we accept about ourselves or reality, and this false belief functions to prevent us from pursuing or accomplishing meaningful goals with excellence. According to Dr. Grimes, we can learn to solve difficulties or discover ways to avoid them, but this is not possible if we are operating with the false belief and problem that he calls the *pathologos* (literally, the "sick belief"). The goal of midwifery is to help discover the origin and maintenance of these beliefs. These beliefs often dominate our lives and establish the patterns and cycles that we repeat and that limit our well-being. It is understandable if we are skeptical that such negative forces in our lives can be resolved simply through understanding the nature of the belief. We may even think that we already know the origin and nature of such a belief and that it does not help us solve our life's difficulties.

Philosophical midwifery works because it awakens us to an understanding that we have never experienced before, to a level of the human mind and its functioning that has remained dormant until the birth of a special form of insight. Philosophical midwifery helps us bring to birth beliefs that we presently hold to be true and learned in our childhoods but that we never expressed in words. It is because these beliefs were never expressed that they have a remarkable power over the human psyche; when they are discovered and put into word, they gain a liberating power. It is the power of this belief that shapes much of our fate, and the power of seeing it releases the providential energy of the mind that will help us realize greater good in our lives.

The following questions are from an article by Dr. Grimes entitled "The Art of Delivering Oneself of False Beliefs."* You may choose to explore these questions on your own or as part of a dialogue with a close friend. It will be important to write the exploration down if you proceed alone. If you choose dialogue, it will be helpful to tape-record it and take notes. Such an exploration will be most beneficial if it follows the principles of dialogue outlined in this book. As you seek understanding, you will also be benefited by considering Paul Brunton's lessons on intuition in the sixth chapter, "The Inner Dialogue."

---

*Grimes, Pierre, "The Art of Delivering Oneself of False Beliefs: Part 2: The Signs of a Problem," *New Perspectives*, 8, No. 3 (1994), pp. 10–13.

State the Nature of Your Problem

1. The first step is to state as clearly as you can the nature of your problem. What reasons do you give yourself for not achieving your highest goals?
2. As you consider these goals and why you have not achieved them, could you explain the effect this failure has had on your life?
3. Again, what is it like when you anticipate facing these problems in your daily life?

Describe the Scenes in the Present and the Recent Past

Take the present difficulty you are having and, as you review it, see if you can determine when it began. Consider the stages it has passed through and see if you can identify just where in those stages you felt most depressed or in a negative state of mind. In the same way, identify the stages where you experienced a "high" and when it was most intense.

1. Choose two or three times in the recent past, say within the past few days or weeks, when you felt down or were not yourself and, after recollecting these events, write them down.
2. Carefully compare and contrast this description with the high and low states you described in the first question. Examine the sequences of the events for their similarities and differences.
3. Can you explain why these intense highs and lows occur? Does the presence of these states of mind signal your problem? Is that what it means to have a problem—to face the consequences of these states of mind?

Recall Early Incidents

Keep your mind on the description you just gave of these states of mind and reflect on the role they have played in your life.

1. Recall early incidents in your life when you experienced these states of mind most intensely. Make notes on your reflections. How old were you then? Who was present? Describe the states of mind of those present.
2. What was said at that time? Try to recall the words as precisely as you can. Can you recall the times when you experienced these same words and expressions as thoughts? What effect do those thoughts have upon you? If the thoughts arise when you are trying to achieve a goal—one that is personally significant to you—do they help or hinder your chance of success?

Note: It sometimes happens that the incident that you recall may not be one in which you experienced the same state of mind as in your present situation, and that is because you may either have experienced someone other than yourself in that particular feeling state or find it difficult or nearly impossible to recall a particular emotional state in your past. If so, consider if it might be that you often experience that state of mind or have experienced it for a long period of time. If this is the case, just choose some time when that state of mind was more intense than at other times. In either case, write down what comes to your mind and continue with your reflections.

Reflect on That Early Scene

It is necessary to reconstruct that early scene in as much detail as possible. Picture the scene again as if you were watching it being rerun or re-enacted. Describe the scene. What impact did it have on you? What effect did it have on the others?

1. *After:* What did you do after the most intense part of the drama? Did you say anything? Where did you go? What did those around you do after they saw this scene take place?
2. *Before:* In the same way, describe what happened before the intense scene that you just described. Go back into your recollections to recall all that you can that preceded that

scene, asking yourself what you and those around you were doing and what was said.

3. *Beginning*: Describe the state of mind you were in as this scene began.

Note: *If you have not recalled a scene when you were living with your parents or when you were a child, go through these same questions, but this time go back to the time when you were younger and living in your parents' home.*

Continue Reflecting

It is essential that you continue reflecting and exploring those scenes until you can recall nothing new. Try these questions to help your recollections. Was there a special scene of discipline? A particular degree of punishment? Was there a fight? Was there an intense argument? A peak of yelling? Or was there no violence, no injury?

1. How was the "making up" scene enacted? Where? What room? Who was there? What was said? What did they and you do?

2. How did you know when it was over? How did you know when you could forget it? How was peace or a truce established?

Chart the Event, Show the Cycle

Chart the event or picture it in terms of a time sequence. See if you can put it into a circle; include all the states, because a problem plays itself out periodically as the cycle of a circle. You can use this chart later as a personal mandala.

Reflect Further

Now you must reflect further on what you have done. Consider these questions.

1. How intense were these scenes? How alert and aware were you, and what of the others who took part in these scenes?

2. Even though it may have been negative, how much concern was shown you? How much attention was focused on you? Were they showing what mattered most to them? How intimate was it?

3. If the worst thing is to be merely tolerated, because we must know how others feel toward us, then how important is this display of emotion and feeling?

4. When there is no crisis, how do the others appear? As real, as powerful, as knowing, and as sincere as during the crisis? Did they or you ever show that much feeling at other times? Can you see why it is at such times that feelings are shown and displayed?

5. Did this event teach you something? Did you learn even though you may have preferred some other lesson?

6. Was the lesson you were learning at that time connected with your being accepted and understood? Was this the time others could show you they care? Does this become the moment when they demonstrate they care?

7. Do you see that this is one way of showing feelings of concern, even of love, because it is difficult to see the genuine marks of love and so we are driven to communicate it in ways in which we were shown love and concern in our own youth?

8. Compare the states of mind when the scene began and during the last episode of that scene. Did you move from better to worse? Does your present state of mind reflect this last episode?

9. How frequently did such scenes occur? Looking back, could you say that you could have or should have been able to predict them? Why?

Reflect Back on the Statement of Your Problem

Reflect on the first stage, the statement of your problem, and consider whether that statement fits the past scene and if it is a better way to understand the past than the present. Could a problem statement made in the present actually be a conclusion or a lesson of something learned from a past scene? Why?

Reflect and Puzzle Out the Meaning

Now that you have written down all that you have seen, it is time to reflect upon it and puzzle out its meaning. If you see the structure or pattern of your problem repeating itself through your life and can realize how it is passed down to each generation, then you have come to acknowledge that this is the cause of your confusion, despair, and suffering. If this is so, can you surmount it? If it is a problem, it can be solved. Study it carefully. Look for more details, find connections, avoid generalities. Watch yourself when you experience similar states of mind and look for similarities to your past. Study yourself and let your present be a mirror through which to emerge from your past. Notice another thing. You may see that you are presently in a role that actually was that of another member of your family, perhaps your father's or mother's. That's right—a problem continues to be played out even when we no longer take the role of child.

A problem is *learned*. We learn from others how to play it; it will survive our death. Just as you learned from your parents, so you will pass it on to those who are intimate with you, unless, of course, you decide to end it now by seeing it fully and consciously. When you feel curious about whether you have really understood a problem, you may find the following questions valuable. What was happening that made the problem surface? What was going on that made its appearance necessary? Clearly, if you don't see that, then it is likely you will return to the problem again because there is still some part that is obscure to you. If this is so, study yourself further, look more closely, talk about it, and you will come to see what has escaped your attention. Thus, the art of delivering oneself of false beliefs must include testing the truth of one's understanding by facing once more those problems in your everyday experience and discovering whether you can now achieve your ideal goals. If you do not succeed with excellence, return again for further analysis and reflection.

Accepting the challenge to answer these questions is the doorway into philosophy—not European or Eastern, but Platonic philosophy. In the process of resolving problems, the most important ideas in philosophy are placed in review: justice, courage, love, understanding, beliefs, and knowing. When we concluded as we did in the early scenes, we accepted the image and shadow of those ideas as real, and those shadows became the *pathologos*. From these early scenes we reached conclusions that became believable because we believed those who appeared to be believable. They seemed to be sincere, noble, knowing, and caring, so that we, in turn, accepted their message. We traded the genuine and real for the false and delusionary, and we passed into the world of false beliefs. When we are in the grip of the *pathologos*, we judge everything through it; in judging through it we are locked into reducing everything to the beliefs of the *pathologos*. And in that reduction we experience an alienation from those most important to us and a sense of futility because we cannot achieve our most cherished dreams and ideals. A *pathologos* blocks us from fulfilling our destiny and makes us live a life without reflection. Our fate becomes a shadow of the real, but we can recover our direction and become a part of a nobler vision that is the true flower of man's destiny.

BIBLIOGRAPHY

Apatow, Robert Charles, "Awakening Plato's Menon: A Translation and Account of the Dialogue as a Whole," (Ph.D. diss., University of Michigan, Ann Arbor, 1993).

Brunton, Paul, *The Wisdom of the Overself* (New York: E. P. Dutton, 1945).

Fowler, H.N., trans., *Plato Volume IV* (Cambridge, Massachusetts: Harvard University Press, 1992).

Grimes, Pierre, and Uliana, Regina, *Philosophical Midwifery: A New Paradigm for Understanding Human Problems with Its Validation* (Costa Mesa, California: Hyparxis Press, 1998).

Grimes, Pierre, *Is It All Relative? A Play on Plato's Theaetetus* (Costa Mesa, California: Hyparxis Press, 1995).

Grimes, Pierre, "The Art of Delivering Oneself of False Beliefs: Part 2: The Signs of a Problem," *New Perspectives*, 8, No. 3 (1994).

Heath, Thomas, trans., *Euclid's Elements of Geometry* (New York: Dover Publications, 1956).

Henrigel, Eugene, *Zen and the Art of Dialogue* (New York: Vintage Press, 1971).

Huizinga, Johan, *Homo Ludens: A Study of the Play Element in Culture* (Boston: Beacon Press, 1955).

Huntington, Samuel P., "The Clash of Civilizations," *Foreign Affairs*, 27, No. 3 (1993), pp. 22–49.

Jackson, Phil, and Delehauy, Hugh, *Sacred Hoops: Spiritual Lessons of a Hardwood Warrior* (New York: Hyperion, 1995).

Lamb, W. R. M., trans., *Plato Volume XIII* (Cambridge, Massachusetts: Harvard University Press, 1986).

Morrow, Glenn R., and Dillon, John M., trans., *Proclus' Commentary on Plato's Parmenides* (Princeton, New Jersey: Princeton University Press, 1987).

Ralston, Peter, *Cheng Hsin: The Principles of Effortless Power* (Berkeley, California: North Atlantic Books, 1989).

Rouse, W. H. D., trans., *Great Dialogues of Plato (Citro)*, (New York: Mentor Press, 1984).

Suzuki, Shunryu, "Zen Mind, Beginner's Mind," (New York: Weatherhill, 1986).

Wick, Gerry Shishin, "Zen in the Workplace: Approaches to Mindful Management," *Tricycle: The Buddhist Review*, 5, No. 4 (1996), p. 14–19.

Yates, Francis A., *The Art of Memory* (Chicago, University of Chicago, 1966).